STATUTES

Evidence

Second Edition

SERIES EDITOR: D G CRACKNELL
EDITOR: D G CRACKNELL
LLB, of the Middle Temple, Barrister

OLD BAILEY PRESS

OLD BAILEY PRESS
200 Greyhound Road, London W14 9RY

First published 1994
Second edition 1997

ISBN 1 85836 065 X

British Library Cataloguing-in-Publication.

A CIP Catalogue record for this book is available from the British Library.

Printed and bound in Great Britain.

CONTENTS

PREFACE

THE rules of evidence are a vitally important part of the judicial process and most of these rules, including numerous exceptions to them, are to be found in Acts of Parliament.

This book contains provisions from fifty-six statutes, in their amended form, with which students are required to be familiar or to which, at least, they will need to refer. In terms of time, they run from the Witnesses Act 1806 (ability to refuse to answer questions) to the Civil Procedure Act 1997. Of course, the Civil Evidence Act 1995 (dealing with, amongst other things, the admissibility of hearsay evidence and the proof of certain documentary evidence) and the Criminal Procedure Investigations Act 1996 are important additions.

Since it is not known when the Act will be brought into force, the relevant provisions of the Sexual Offences (Protected Materials) Act 1997 are included in the Appendix.

Amendments or substitutions made on or before 1 August 1997 have been taken into account and the source of any changes is noted at the end of a particular statute. The text assumes that the Criminal Procedure and Investigations Act 1996 is fully in force, but at 1 August commencement dates were awaited for ss45, 49, 62, 66 and 67 and this is noted in appropriate places.

ALPHABETICAL TABLE OF STATUTES

WITNESSES ACT 1806

(46 Geo 3 c 37)

1 Witnesses cannot refuse to answer questions tending to establish their indebtedness, etc

A witness cannot by law refuse to answer a question relevant to the matter in issue, the answering of which has no tendency to accuse himself or to expose him to penalty or forfeiture of any nature whatsoever, by reason only or on the sole ground that the answering of such question may establish or tend to establish that he owes a debt, or is otherwise subject to a civil suit either at the instance of His Majesty or of any other person or persons.

EVIDENCE ACT 1845

(8 & 9 Vict c 113)

1 Certain documents purporting to be sealed, signed, etc to be received in evidence without proof of seal or signature, etc of person signing the same, where the original record could have been received

Whenever by any Act now in force or hereafter to be in force any certificate, official or public document, or document or proceedings of any corporation or joint stock or other company, or any certified copy of any document, bye law, entry in any register or other book, or of any other proceeding, shall be receivable in evidence of any particular in any court of justice, or before any legal tribunal, or either House of Parliament, or any committee of either House, or in any judicial proceeding, the same shall respectively be admitted in evidence, provided they respectively purport to be sealed or impressed with a stamp or sealed and signed, or signed alone, as required, or impressed with a stamp and signed, as directed by the respective Acts made or to be hereafter made, without any proof of the seal or stamp, where a seal or stamp is necessary, or of the signature or of the official character of the person appearing to have signed the same, and without any further proof thereof, in every case in which the original record could have been received in evidence.

2 Courts, etc to take judicial notice of signature of equity or common law judges, attached to decrees, etc

All courts, judges, justices, masters in chancery, masters of courts, commissioners judicially acting, and other judicial officers, shall henceforth take judicial notice of the signature of any of the equity or common law judges of the superior courts at Westminster, provided such signature be attached or appended to any decree, order, certificate, or other judicial or official document.

3 Queen's printers' copies of private Acts, etc admissible

All copies of private and local and personal Acts of Parliament not public Acts, if purporting to be printed by the Queen's printers, and all copies of the journals of either House of Parliament, and of royal proclamations, purporting to be printed by the printers to the crown or by the printers to either House of Parliament, or by any or either of them, shall be admitted as evidence thereof by all courts, judges, justices, and others without any proof being given that such copies were so printed.

As amended by the Statute Law Revision Act 1891.

EVIDENCE ACT 1851

(14 & 15 Vict c 99)

2 Parties to be admissible witnesses

On the trial of any issue joined, or of any matter or question, or on any inquiry arising in any suit, action, or other proceeding in any court of justice, or before any person having by law, or by consent of parties, authority to hear, receive, and examine evidence, the parties thereto, and the persons in whose behalf any such suit, action, or other proceeding may be brought or defended, shall, except as hereinafter excepted, be competent and compellable to give evidence, either viva voce or by deposition, according to the practice of the court, on behalf of either or any of the parties to the said suit, action, or other proceeding.

3 Saving as to criminal proceedings

But nothing herein contained shall render any person who in any criminal proceeding is charged with the commission of any indictable offence, or any offence punishable on summary conviction, competent or compellable to give evidence for or against himself or herself, or shall render any person compellable to answer any question tending to criminate himself or herself, or shall in any criminal proceeding render any husband competent or compellable to give evidence for or against his wife, or any wife competent or compellable to give evidence for or against her husband.

7 Proof of foreign and colonial acts of state, judgments, etc

All proclamations, treaties, and other acts of state of any foreign state or of any British colony, and all judgments, decrees, orders, and other judicial proceedings of any court of justice in any foreign state or in any British colony, and all affidavits, pleadings, and other legal documents filed or deposited in any such court, may be proved in any court of justice, or before any person having by law or by consent of parties authority to hear, receive, and examine evidence, either by examined copies or by copies authenticated as herein-after mentioned; that is to say, if the document sought to be proved be a proclamation, treaty, or other act of state, the authenticated copy to be admissible in evidence must purport to be sealed with the seal of the foreign state or British colony to which the original document belongs; and if the document sought to be proved be a judgment, decree, order, or other judicial proceeding of any foreign or colonial court, or an affidavit, pleading, or other legal document filed or deposited in any such court, the authenticated copy to be admissible in evidence must purport either to be sealed with the seal of the foreign or colonial court to which the original document belongs, or, in the event of such court having no seal, to be signed by the judge, or, if there be more than one judge, by any one of the judges of the said court; and such judge shall attach to his signature a statement in writing on the said copy that the court whereof he is a judge has no seal; but if any of the aforesaid authenticated copies shall purport to be sealed or signed as herein-before respectively directed, the same shall respectively be admitted in evidence in every case in which the original document could have been received in evidence, without any proof of the seal where a seal is necessary, or of the signature, or of the truth of the statement attached thereto, where such signature and statement are necessary, or of the judicial character of the person appearing to have made such signature and statement.

14 Examined or certified copies or extracts of public documents to be admissible in evidence

Whenever any book or other document is of such a public nature as to be admissible in evidence on its mere production from the proper custody, and no statute exists which renders its contents provable by means of a copy, any copy thereof or extract therefrom shall be admissible in evidence in any court of justice, or before any person now or hereafter having by law or by consent of parties authority to hear, receive, and examine evidence, provided it be proved to be an examined copy or extract, or provided it purport to be signed and certified as a true copy or extract by the officer to whose custody the original is intrusted, and which officer is hereby required to furnish such certified copy or extract to any person applying at a reasonable time for the same, upon payment of a reasonable sum for the same, not exceeding fourpence for every folio of ninety words.

16 Administration of oaths

Every court, judge, justice, officer, commissioner, arbitrator, or other person, now or hereafter having by law or by consent of parties authority to hear, receive, and examine evidence, is hereby empowered to administer an oath to all such witnesses as are legally called before them respectively.

EVIDENCE AMENDMENT ACT 1853
(16 & 17 Vict c 83)

1 Husbands and wives of parties to be admissible witnesses

On the trial of any issue joined, or of any matter or question, or on any inquiry arising in any suit, action, or other proceeding in any court of justice, or before any person having by law or by consent of parties authority to hear, receive, and examine evidence, the husbands and wives of the parties thereto, and of the persons in whose behalf any such suit, action, or other proceedings may be brought or instituted, or opposed or defended, shall, except as hereinafter expected, be competent and compellable to give evidence, either viva voce or by deposition, according to the practice of the court, on behalf of either or any of the parties to the said suit, action, or other proceeding.

2 Saving as to criminal cases

Nothing herein shall render any husband competent or compellable to give evidence for or against his wife, or any wife competent or compellable to give evidence for or against her husband, in any criminal proceeding.

As amended by the Evidence Further Amendment Act 1869, s1.

CRIMINAL PROCEDURE ACT 1865

(28 & 29 Vict c 18)

1 Sections 3 to 8 to [apply to] all courts and persons authorised to hear evidence

The provisions of sections from 3 to 8, inclusive, of this Act shall apply to all courts of judicature, as well as criminal as all others, and to all persons having, by law or by consent of parties, authority to hear, receive, and examine evidence.

2 Summing up of evidence in cases of felony and misdemeanor

If any prisoner or prisoners, defendant or defendants, shall be defended by counsel, but not otherwise, it shall be the duty of the presiding judge, at the close of the case for the prosecution, to ask the counsel for each prisoner or defendant so defended by counsel whether he or they intend to adduce evidence; and in the event of none of them thereupon announcing his intention to adduce evidence, the counsel for the prosecution shall be allowed to address the jury a second time in support of his case, for the purpose of summing up the evidence against such prisoner or prisoners, or defendant or defendants; and upon every trial, whether the prisoners or defendants, or any of them, shall be defended by counsel or not, each and every such prisoner or defendant, or his or their counsel respectively, shall be allowed, if he or they shall think fit, to open his or their case or cases respectively; and after the conclusion of such opening or of all such openings, if more than one, such prisoner or prisoners, or defendant or defendants, or their counsel, shall be entitled to examine such witnesses as he or they may think fit, and when all the evidence is concluded to sum up the evidence respectively; and the right of reply, and practice and course of proceedings, save as hereby altered, shall be as at present.

3 How far witnesses may be discredited by the party producing

A party producing a witness shall not be allowed to impeach his credit by general evidence of bad character; but he may, in case the witness shall in the opinion of the judge prove adverse, contradict him by other evidence, or, by leave of the judge, prove that he has made at other times a statement inconsistent with his present testimony; but before such last-mentioned proof can be given the circumstances of the supposed statement, sufficient to designate the particular occasion, must be mentioned to the witness, and he must be asked whether or not he has made such statement.

4 As to proof of contradictory statements of adverse witness

If a witness, upon cross-examination as to a former statement made by him relative to the subject matter of the indictment or proceeding, and inconsistent with his present testimony, does not distinctly admit that he has made such statement, proof may be given that he did in fact make it; but before such proof can be given the circumstances of the supposed statement, sufficient to designate the particular occasion, must be mentioned to the witness, and he must be asked whether or not he has made such statement.

5 Cross-examinations as to previous statements in writing

A witness may be cross-examined as to previous statements made by him in writing, or reduced into writing, relative to the subject matter of the indictment or proceeding, without such writing being shown to him; but if it is intended to contradict such witness by the writing, his attention must, before such contradictory proof can be given, be called to those parts of the writing which are to be used for the purpose of so contradicting him: provided always, that it shall be competent for the judge, at any time during the trial, to require the production of the writing for his inspection, and he may thereupon make such use of it for the purposes of the trial as he may think fit.

6 Proof of conviction of witness for felony or misdemeanour may be given

A witness may be questioned as to whether he has been convicted of any felony or misdemeanour, and upon being so questioned, if he either denies or does not admit the fact, or refuses to answer, it shall be lawful for the cross-examining party to prove such conviction; and a certificate containing the substance and effect only (omitting the formal part) of the indictment and conviction for such offence, purporting to be signed by the clerk of the court or other officer having the custody of the records of the court where the offender was convicted, or by the deputy of such clerk or officer (for which certificate a fee of 25p and no more shall be demanded or taken), shall, upon proof of the identity of the person, be sufficient evidence of the said conviction, without proof of the signature or official character of the person appearing to have signed the same.

7 Proof of instrument to validity of which whereof attestation is not necessary

It shall not be necessary to prove by the attesting witness any instrument to the validity of which attestation is not requisite, and such instrument may be proved as if there had been no attesting witness thereto.

8 Comparison of disputed writing with writing proved to be genuine

Comparison of a disputed writing with any writing proved to the satisfaction of the judge to be genuine shall be permitted to be made by witnesses; and such writings, and the evidence of witnesses respecting the same, may be submitted to the court and jury as evidence of the genuineness or otherwise of the writing in dispute.

9 'Counsel'

The word 'counsel' in this Act shall be construed to apply to attorneys in all cases where attorneys are allowed by law or by the practice of any court to appear as advocates.

NB In s6, the words 'and a certificate' to the end were repealed, in relation to criminal proceedings, by the Police and Criminal Evidence Act 1984, ss119(2), (3), 120, Schedule 7, Pt IV.

As amended by the Statute Law Revision Act 1893; Criminal Law Act 1967, s10(2), Schedule 3, Pt III.

DOCUMENTARY EVIDENCE ACT 1868

(31 & 32 Vict c 37)

2 Mode of proving certain documents

Prima facie evidence of any proclamation, order, or regulation issued before or after the passing of this Act by Her Majesty, or by the Privy Council, also of any proclamation, order, or regulation issued before or after the passing of this Act by or under the authority of any such department of the Government or officer as is mentioned in the first column of the schedule hereto, may be given in all courts of justice, and in all legal proceedings whatsoever, in all or any of modes hereinafter mentioned; that is to say:

(1) By the production of a copy of the Gazette purporting to contain such proclamation, order, or regulation.

(2) By the production of a copy of such proclamation, order, or regulation, purporting to be printed by the Government printer, or, where the question arises in a court in any British colony or possession, of a copy purporting to be printed under the authority of the legislature of such British colony or possession.

(3) By the production, in the case of any proclamation, order, or regulation issued by Her Majesty or by the Privy Council, of a copy or extract purporting to be certified to be true by the clerk of the Privy Council, or by any one of the lords or others of the Privy Council, and, in the case of any proclamation, order, or regulation issued by or under the authority of any of the said departments or officers, by the production of a copy or extract purporting to be certified to be true by the person or persons specified in the second column of the said schedule in connexion with such department or officer.

Any copy or extract made in pursuance of this Act may be in print or in writing, or partly in print and partly in writing.

No proof shall be required of the handwriting or official position of any person certifying, in pursuance of this Act, to the truth of any copy of or extract from any proclamation, order, or regulation.

5 Interpretation

(1) The following words shall in this Act have the meaning hereinafter assigned to them, unless there is something in the context repugnant to such construction; (that is to say),

'British colony and possession' shall for the purposes of this Act include the Channel Islands, the Isle of Man, and all other Her Majesty's dominions.

'Legislature' shall signify any authority, other than the Imperial Parliament or Her Majesty in Council, competent to make laws for any colony or possession.

'Privy Council' shall include Her Majesty in Council and the lords and others of Her Majesty's Privy Council, or any of them, and any committee of the Privy Council that is not specially named in the schedule hereto.

'Government printer' shall mean and include the printer to Her Majesty, and any printer purporting to be the printer authorised to print the statutes, ordnances, acts of state, or other public acts of the legislature of any British colony or possession, or otherwise to be the Government printer of such colony or possession.

'Gazette' shall include the London Gazette, the Edinburgh Gazette, and the Dublin Gazette, or any of such Gazettes.

6 Provisions of Act to be cumulative

The provisions of this Act shall be deemed to be in addition to, and not in derogation of, any powers of proving documents given by any existing statute, or existing at common law.

SCHEDULE

Column 1 Name of Department or Officer	Column 2 Names of Certifying Officers
The Treasury	Any Commissioner, Secretary, or Assistant Secretary of the Treasury
The Commissioners for executing the office of Lord High Admiral	Any of the Commissioners for executing the office of Lord High Admiral, or either of the Secretaries to the said Commissioners
Secretaries of State	Any Secretary or Under-Secretary of State
Committee of Privy Council for Trade	Any member of the Committee of Privy Council for Trade, or any Secretary or Assistant Secretary of the said Committee
Charity Commissioners for England and Wales	Any Commissioner or Assistant Commissioner and any officer authorised to act on behalf of the Commissioners
The Rail Regulator and the Director of Passenger Rail Franchising	The Regulator, the Franchising Director and any person authorised to act on behalf of the Regulator or the Franchising Director

As amended by the Statute Law Revision Act 1893; the Statute Law (Repeals) Act 1989; Charities Act 1993, s1, Schedule 1, para 3(2); Railways Act 1993, s1, Schedule 1 para 6(a), (b).

BANKERS' BOOKS EVIDENCE ACT 1879

(42 & 43 Vict c 11)

3 Mode of proof of entries in bankers' books

Subject to the provisions of this Act, a copy of any entry in a banker's book shall in all legal proceedings be received as prima facie evidence of such entry, and of the matters, transactions, and accounts therein recorded.

4 Proof that book is a banker's book

A copy of an entry in a banker's book shall not be received in evidence under this Act unless it be first proved that the book was at the time of the making of the entry one of the ordinary books of the bank, and that the entry was made in the usual and ordinary course of business, and that the book is in the custody or control of the bank.

Such proof may be given by a partner or officer of the bank, and may be given orally or by an affidavit sworn before any commissioner or person authorised to take affidavits.

Where the proceedings concerned are proceedings before a magistrates' court inquiring into an offence as examining justices, this section shall have effect with the omission of the words 'orally or'.

5 Verification of copy

A copy of an entry in a banker's book shall not be received in evidence under this Act unless it be further proved that the copy has been examined with the original entry and is correct.

Such proof shall be given by some person who has examined the copy with the original entry, and may be given either orally or by an affidavit sworn before any commissioner or person authorised to take affidavits.

Where the proceedings concerned are proceedings before a magistrates' court inquiring into an offence as examining justices, this section shall have effect with the omission of the words 'either orally or'.

6 Case in which banker, etc not compellable to produce book, etc

A banker or officer of a bank shall not, in any legal proceedings to which the bank is not a party, be compellable to produce any banker's book the contents of which can be proved under this Act ..., or to appear as a witness to prove the matters, transactions, and accounts therein recorded, unless by order of a judge made for special cause.

7 Court or judge may order inspection, etc

On the application of any party to a legal proceeding a court or judge may order that such party be at liberty to inspect and take copies of any entries in a banker's book for any of the purposes of such proceedings. An order under this section may be made either with or without summoning the bank or any other party, and shall be served on the bank three clear days before the same is to be obeyed, unless the court or judge otherwise directs.

8 Costs

The costs of any application to a court or judge under or for the purposes of this Act, and the costs of anything done or to be done under an order of a court or judge made under or for the purposes of this Act shall be in the discretion of the court or judge, who may order the same or any part thereof to be paid to any party by the bank, where the same have been occasioned by any default or delay on the part of the bank. Any such order against a bank may be enforced as if the bank was a party to the proceeding.

9 Interpretation of 'bank', 'banker', and 'bankers' books'

(1) In this Act the expressions 'bank' and 'banker' mean –

(a) an institution authorised under the Banking Act 1987 or a municipal bank within the meaning of that Act;

(aa) a building society (within the meaning of the Building Societies Act 1986);

(c) the National Savings Bank; and

(d) the Post office, in the exercise of its powers to provide banking services.

(2) Expressions in this Act relating to 'bankers' books' include ledgers, day books, cash books, account books and other records used in the ordinary business of the bank, whether those records are in written form or are kept

on microfilm, magnetic tape or any other form of mechanical or electronic data retrieval mechanism.

10 Interpretation of 'legal proceeding', 'court', 'judge'

In this Act –

The expression 'legal proceeding' means any civil or criminal proceeding or inquiry in which evidence is or may be given, and includes an arbitration and an application to, or an inquiry or other proceeding before, the Solicitors Disciplinary Tribunal ...

The expression 'the court' means the court, judge, arbitrator, persons or person before whom a legal proceeding is held or taken;

The expression 'a judge' means with respect to England a judge of the High Court; ...

The judge of a county court may with respect to any action in such court exercise the powers of a judge under this Act.

11 Computation of time

Sunday, Christmas Day, Good Friday, and any bank holiday shall be excluded from the computation of time under this Act.

As amended by the Statute Law Revision Act 1898; Solicitors Act 1974, s86; Banking Act 1979, s51(1), Schedule 6, Pt I, para 1, Pt II, para 13; Building Societies Act 1986, s120(1), Schedule 18, Pt I, para 1; Banking Act 1987, s108(1), Schedule 6, para 1; Criminal Procedure and Investigations Act 1996, s47, Schedule 1, Pt II, paras 15, 16.

DOCUMENTARY EVIDENCE ACT 1882

(45 & 46 Vict c 9)

2 Documents printed under superintendence of Stationery Office receivable in evidence

Where any enactment, whether passed before or after the passing of this Act, provides that a copy of any Act of Parliament, proclamation, order, regulation, rule, warrant, circular, list, gazette, or document shall be conclusive evidence, or be evidence, or have any other effect, when purporting to be printed by the Government Printer, or the Queen's Printer, or a printer authorised by Her Majesty, or otherwise under Her Majesty's authority, whatever may be the precise expression used, such copy shall also be conclusive evidence, or have the said effect (as the case may be) if it purports to be printed under the superintendence or authority of Her Majesty's Stationery Office.

STAMP ACT 1891
(54 & 55 Vict c 39)

12 Assessment of duty by Commissioners

(5) Every instrument stamped with the particular stamp denoting either that it is not chargeable with any duty, or is duly stamped, shall be admissible in evidence, and available for all purposes notwithstanding any objection relating to duty.

(6) Provided as follows: ...

(b) Nothing in this section shall authorise the stamping after the execution thereof of any instrument which by law cannot be stamped after execution. ...

14 Terms upon which instruments not duly stamped may be received in evidence

(1) Upon the production of an instrument chargeable with any duty as evidence in any court of civil judicature in any part of the United Kingdom, or before any arbitrator or referee, notice shall be taken by the judge arbitrator, or referee of any omission or insufficiency of the stamp thereon, and if the instrument is one which may legally be stamped after the execution thereof, it may, on payment to the officer of the court whose duty it is to read the instrument, or to the arbitrator or referee, of the amount of the unpaid duty, and the penalty payable on stamping the same, and of a further sum of one pound, be received in evidence, saving all just exceptions on other grounds.

(2) The officer, or arbitrator, or referee receiving the duty and penalty shall give a receipt for the same, and make an entry in a book kept for that purpose of the payment and of the amount thereof, and shall communicate to the Commissioners the name or title of the proceedings in which, and of the party from whom, he received the duty and penalty, and the date and description of the instrument, and shall pay over to such person as the Commissioners may appoint the money received by him for the duty and penalty.

(3) On production to the Commissioners of any instrument in respect of which any duty or penalty has been paid, together with the receipt, the payment of the duty and penalty shall be denoted on the instrument.

(4) Save as aforesaid, an instrument executed in any part of the United Kingdom, or relating, wheresoever executed, to any property situate, or to any matter or thing done or to be done, in any part of the United Kingdom, shall not, except in criminal proceedings, be given in evidence, or be available for any purpose whatever, unless it is duly stamped in accordance with the law in force at the time when it was first executed.

As amended by the Finance Act 1971, s69, Schedule 14, Pt VI.

DOCUMENTARY EVIDENCE ACT 1895

(58 & 59 Vict c 9)

1 Application of Documentary Evidence Acts to Board of Agriculture

The Documentary Evidence Act 1868, as amended by the Documentary Evidence Act 1882, shall apply to the Board of Agriculture in like manner as if that Board were mentioned in the first column of the schedule to the first-mentioned Act, and the President or any member of the Board, or the Secretary of the Board, or any person authorised by the President to act on behalf of the Secretary of the Board, were mentioned in the second column of that schedule, and as if the regulations referred to in those Acts included any document issued by the Board.

CRIMINAL EVIDENCE ACT 1898

(61 & 62 Vict c 36)

1 Competency of witnesses in criminal cases

Every person charged with an offence shall be a competent witness for the defence at every stage of the proceedings, whether the person so charged is charged solely or jointly with any other person. Provided as follows –

(a) A person so charged shall not be called as a witness in pursuance of this Act except upon his own application;

(e) A person charged and being a witness in pursuance of this Act may be asked any question in cross-examination notwithstanding that it would tend to criminate him as to the offence charged;

(f) A person charged and called as a witness in pursuance of this Act shall not be asked, and if asked shall not be required to answer, any question tending to show that he has committed or been convicted of or been charged with any offence other than that wherewith he is then charged, or is of bad character, unless –

(i) the proof that he has committed or been convicted of such other offence is admissible evidence to show that he is guilty of the offence wherewith he is then charged; or

(ii) he has personally or by his advocate asked questions of the witnesses for the prosecution with a view to establish his own good character, or has given evidence of his good character, or the nature or conduct of the defence is such as to involve imputations on the character of the prosecutor or the witnesses for the prosecution or the deceased victim of the alleged crime; or

(iii) he has given evidence against any other person charged in the same proceedings.

(g) Every person called as a witness in pursuance of this Act shall, unless otherwise ordered by the court, give his evidence from the witness box or other place from which the other witnesses give their evidence.

2 Evidence of person charged

Where the only witness to the facts of the case called by the defence is the person charged, he shall be called as a witness immediately after the close of the evidence for the prosecution.

As amended by the Criminal Evidence Act 1979, s1; Criminal Justice Act 1982, s78, Schedule 16; Police and Criminal Evidence Act 1984, ss80(9), 119(2), Schedule 7, Pt V; Criminal Justice and Public Order Act 1994, ss31, 168(2), (3), Schedule 10, para 2.

PERJURY ACT 1911

(1 & 2 Geo 5 c 6)

13 Corroboration

A person shall not be liable to be convicted of any offence against this Act, or of any offence declared by any other Act to be perjury or subornation of perjury, or to be punishable as perjury or subornation of perjury, solely upon the evidence of one witness as to the falsity of any statement alleged to be false.

OFFICIAL SECRETS ACT 1911

(1 & 2 Geo 5 c 28)

1 Penalties for spying

(1) If any person for any purpose prejudicial to the safety or interests of the State –

(a) approaches, inspects, passes over or is in the neighbourhood of, or enters any prohibited place within the meaning of this Act; or

(b) makes any sketch, plan, model, or note which is calculated to be or might be or is intended to be directly or indirectly useful to an enemy; or

(c) obtains, collects, records, or publishes, or communicates to any other person any secret official code word or pass word, or any sketch, plan, model, article, or note, or other document or information which is calculated to be or might be or is intended to be directly useful to an enemy;

he shall be guilty of felony.

(2) On a prosecution under this section, it shall not be necessary to show that the accused person was guilty of any particular act tending to show a purpose prejudicial to the safety or interests of the State, and, notwithstanding that no such act is proved against him, he may be convicted if, from the circumstances of the case, or his conduct, or his known character as proved, it appears that his purpose was a purpose prejudicial to the safety or interests of the State; and if any sketch, plan, model, article, note, document, or information relating to or used in any prohibited place within the meaning of this Act, or anything in such a place or any secret official code word or pass word, is made, obtained, collected, recorded, published, or communicated by any person other than a person acting under lawful authority, it shall be deemed to have been made, obtained, collected, recorded, published or communicated for a purpose prejudicial to the safety or interests of the State unless the contrary is proved.

As amended by the Official Secrets Act 1920, ss10, 11(2), Schedules 1, 2.

PREVENTION OF CORRUPTION ACT 1916

(6 & 7 Geo 5 c 64)

2 Presumption of corruption in certain cases

Where in any proceedings against a person for an offence under the Prevention of Corruption Act 1906, or the Public Bodies Corrupt Practices Act 1889, it is proved that any money, gift, or other consideration has been paid or given to or received by a person in the employment of His Majesty or any Government Department or a public body by or from a person, or agent of a person, holding or seeking to obtain a contract from His Majesty or any Government Department or public body, the money, gift, or consideration shall be deemed to have been paid or given and received corruptly as such inducement or reward as is mentioned in such Act unless the contrary is proved.

4 Short title and interpretation

(2) In this Act and in the Public Bodies Corrupt Practices Act 1889, the expression 'public body' includes, in addition to the bodies mentioned in the last-mentioned Act, local and public authorities of all descriptions.

LAW OF PROPERTY ACT 1925

(15 & 16 Geo 5 c 20)

184 Presumption of survivorship in regard to claims to property

In all cases where, after the commencement of this Act, two or more persons have died in circumstances rendering it uncertain which of them survived the other or others, such deaths shall (subject to any order of the court), for all purposes affecting the title of property, be presumed to have occurred in order of seniority, and accordingly the younger shall be deemed to have survived the elder.

CHILDREN AND YOUNG PERSONS ACT 1933

(22 Geo 5 c 12)

4 Causing or allowing persons under sixteen to be used for begging

(1) If any person causes or procures any child or young person under the age of sixteen years or, having responsibility for such a child or young person, allows him to be in any street, premises, or place for the purpose of begging or receiving alms, or of inducing the giving of alms (whether or not there is any pretence of singing, playing, performing, offering anything for sale, or otherwise), he shall, on summary conviction, be liable to a fine not exceeding level 2 on the standard scale, or alternatively, or in addition thereto, to imprisonment for any term not exceeding three months.

(2) If a person having responsibility for a child or young person is charged with an offence under this section, and it is proved that the child or young person was in any street, premises, or place for any such purpose as aforesaid, and that the person charged allowed the child or young person to be in the street, premises, or place, he shall be presumed to have allowed him to be in the street, premises, or place for that purpose unless the contrary is proved.

(3) If any person while singing, playing, performing or offering anything for sale in a street or public place has with him a child who has been lent or hired out to him, the child shall, for the purposes of this section, be deemed to be in that street or place for the purpose of inducing the giving of alms.

42 Extension of power to take deposition of child or young person

(1) Where a justice of the peace is satisfied by the evidence of a duly qualified medical practitioner that the attendance before the court of any child or young person in respect of whom any of the offences mentioned in the First Schedule to this Act is alleged to have been committed would

involve serious damage to his life or health, the justice may take in writing the deposition of the child or young person on oath, and shall thereupon subscribe the deposition and add thereto a statement of his reason for taking it and of the day when and place where it was taken, and of the names of the persons (if any) present at the taking thereof.

(2) The justice taking any such deposition shall transmit it with his statement –

(a) if the deposition relates to an offence for which any accused person is already committed for trial, to the proper officer of the court at which the accused person has been committed; and

(b) in any other case, to the clerk of the court before which proceedings are pending in respect of the offence.

43 Admission of deposition of child or young person in evidence

Where, in any proceedings in respect of any of the offences mentioned in the First Schedule to this Act, the court is satisfied by the evidence of a duly qualified medical practitioner that the attendance before the court of any child or young person in respect of whom the offence is alleged to have been committed would involve serious danger to his life or health, any deposition of the child or young person taken under the Indictable Offences Act 1848, or this Part of this Act, shall be admissible in evidence either for or against the accused person without further proof thereof if it purports to be signed by the justice by or before whom it purports to be taken:

Provided that the deposition shall not be admissible in evidence against the accused person unless it is proved that reasonable notice of the intention to take the deposition has been served upon him and that he or his counsel or solicitor had, or might have had if he had chosen to be present, an opportunity of cross-examining the child or young person making the deposition.

50 Age of criminal responsibility

It shall be conclusively presumed that no child under the age of ten years can be guilty of any offence.

99 Presumption and determination of age

(1) Where a person, whether charged with an offence or not, is brought before any court otherwise than for the purpose of giving evidence, and it appears to the court that he is a child or young person, the court shall make

due inquiry as to the age of that person, and for that purpose shall take such evidence as may be forthcoming at the hearing of the case, but an order or judgement of the court shall not be invalidated by any subsequent proof that the age of that person has not been correctly stated to the court, and the age presumed or declared by the court to be the age of the person so brought before it shall, for the purposes of this Act, be deemed to be the true age of that person, and, whether it appears to the court that the person so brought before it has attained the age of seventeen years, that person shall for the purposes of this Act be deemed not to be a child or young person.

(2) Where in any charge or indictment for any offence under this Act or any of the offences mentioned in the First Schedule to this Act, except as provided in that Schedule, it is alleged that the person by or in respect of whom the offence was committed was a child or young person or was under or had attained any specified age, and he appears to the court to have been at the date of the commission of the alleged offence a child or young person, or to have been under or to have attained the specified age, as the case may be, he shall for the purposes of this Act be presumed at that date to have been a child or young person or to have been under or to have attained that age, as the case may be, unless the contrary is proved.

(3) Where, in any charge or indictment for any offence under this Act or any of the offences mentioned in the First Schedule to this Act, it is alleged that the person in respect of whom the offence was committed was a child or was a young person, it shall not be a defence to prove that the person alleged to have been a child was a young person or the person alleged to have been a young person was a child in any case where the acts constituting the alleged offence would equally have been an offence if committed in respect of a young person or child respectively.

(4) Where a person is charged with an offence under this Act in respect of a person apparently under a specified age it shall be a defence to prove that the person was actually of or over that age.

FIRST SCHEDULE

OFFENCES AGAINST CHILDREN AND YOUNG PERSONS, WITH RESPECT TO WHICH SPECIAL PROVISIONS OF THIS ACT APPLY

The murder or manslaughter of a child or young person.

Infanticide.

Any offence under sections 27 or 56 of the Offences against the Person Act 1861, and any offence against a child or young person under section 5 of that Act.

Common assault, or battery.

Any offence under sections 1, 3, 4, 11 or 23 of this Act.

Any offence against a child or young person under any of the following sections of the Sexual Offences Act 1956, that is to say sections 2 to 7, 10 to 16, 19, 20, 22 to 26 and 28, and any attempt to commit against a child or young person an offence under sections 2, 5, 6, 7, 10, 11, 12, 22 or 23 of that Act:

Provided that for the purposes of subsection (2) of section 99 of this Act this entry shall apply so far only as it relates to offences under sections 10, 11, 12, 14, 15, 16, 20 and 28 of the Sexual Offences Act 1956, and attempts to commit offences under sections 10, 11 and 12 of that Act.

Any other offence involving bodily injury to a child or young person.

As amended by the Sexual offences Act 1956, ss48, 51, Schedules 3, 4; Children and Young Persons Act 1963, s64(1), (3), Schedule 3, para 4, Schedule 5; Criminal Justice Act 1982, s46; Criminal Justice Act 1988, s170(1), (2), Schedule 15, para 8, Schedule 16; Children Act 1989, s108(5), Schedule 13, paras 2, 3(b).

EVIDENCE ACT 1938

(1 & 2 Geo 6 c 28)

3 Proof of instrument to validity of which attestation is necessary

Subject as hereinafter provided, in any proceedings, whether civil or criminal, an instrument to the validity of which attestation is requisite may, instead of being proved by an attesting witness, be proved in the manner in which it might be proved if no attesting witness were alive:

Provided that nothing in this section shall apply to the proof of wills or other testamentary documents.

4 Presumptions as to documents twenty years old

In any proceedings, whether civil or criminal, there shall, in the case of a document proved, or purporting, to be not less than twenty years old, be made any presumption which immediately before the commencement of this Act would have been made in the case of a document of like character proved, or purporting, to be not less than thirty years old.

PREVENTION OF CRIME ACT 1953

(1 & 2 Eliz 2 c 14)

1 Prohibition of the carrying of offensive weapons without lawful authority or reasonable excuse

(1) Any person who without lawful authority or reasonable excuse, the proof whereof shall lie on him, has with him in any public place any offensive weapon shall be guilty of an offence ...

HOMICIDE ACT 1957

(5 & 6 Eliz 2 c 11)

2 Persons suffering from diminished responsibility

(1) Where a person kills or is a party to the killing of another, he shall not be convicted of murder if he was suffering from such abnormality of mind (whether arising from a condition of arrested or retarded development of mind or any inherent causes or induced by disease or injury) as substantially impaired his mental responsibility for his acts and omissions in doing or being a party to the killing.

(2) On a charge of murder, it shall be for the defence to prove that the person charged is by virtue of this section not liable to be convicted of murder ...

3 Provocation

Where on a charge of murder there is evidence on which the jury can find that the person charged was provoked (whether by things done or by things said or by both together) to lose his self-control, the question whether the provocation was enough to make a reasonable man do as he did shall be left to be determined by the jury; and in determining that question the jury shall take into account everything both done and said according to the effect which, in their opinion, it would have on a reasonable man.

4 Suicide pacts

(1) It shall be manslaughter, and shall not be murder, for a person acting in pursuance of a suicide pact between him and another to kill the other or be a party to the other being killed by a third person.

(2) Where it is shown that a person charged with the murder of another killed the other or was a party to his being killed, it shall be for the defence to prove that the person charged was acting in pursuance of a suicide pact between him and the other.

(3) For the purposes of this section 'suicide pact' means a common agreement between two or more persons having for its object the death of all

of them, whether or not each is to take his own life, but nothing done by a person who enters into a suicide pact shall be treated as done by him in pursuance of the pact unless it is done while he has the settled intention of dying in pursuance of the pact.

As amended by the Suicide Act 1961, s3(2), Schedule 2.

PUBLIC RECORDS ACT 1958

(6 & 7 Eliz 2 c 51)

9 Legal validity of public records and authenticated copies

(2) A copy of or extract from a public record in the Public Record Office purporting to be examined and certified as true and authentic by the proper officer and to be sealed or stamped with the seal of the Public Record office shall be admissible as evidence in any proceedings without any further or other proof thereof if the original record would have been admissible as evidence in those proceedings.

In this subsection the reference to the proper officer is a reference to the Keeper of the Public Records or any other officer of the Public Record office authorised in that behalf by the Keeper of Public Records, and, in the case of copies and extracts made before the commencement of this Act, the deputy keeper of the records or any assistant record keeper appointed under the Public Record Office Act 1838.

CHILDREN AND YOUNG PERSONS ACT 1963

(1963 c 37)

16 Offences committed by children

(2) In any proceedings for an offence committed or alleged to have been committed by a person of or over the age of twenty-one, any offence of which he was found guilty while under the age of fourteen shall be disregarded for the purposes of any evidence relating to his previous convictions; and he shall not be asked, and if asked shall not be required to answer, any question relating to such an offence, notwithstanding that the question would otherwise be admissible under section 1 of the Criminal Evidence Act 1898.

26 Medical evidence by certificate

In any proceedings, other than proceedings for an offence, before a youth court, and on any appeal from a decision of a youth court in any such proceedings, any document purporting to be a certificate of a fully registered medical practitioner as to any person's physical or mental condition shall be admissible as evidence of that condition.

28 Form of oath for use in youth courts and by children and young persons in other courts

(1) Subject to subsection (2) of this section, in relation to any oath administered to and taken by any person before a youth court or administered to and taken by any child or young person before any other court, section 1 of the Oaths Act 1978 shall have effect as if the words 'I promise before Almighty God' were set out in it instead of the words 'I swear by Almighty God that'.

(2) Where in any oath otherwise duly administered and taken either of the forms mentioned in this section is used instead of the other, the oath shall nevertheless be deemed to have been duly administered and taken.

As amended by the Oaths Act 1978, s2; Criminal Justice Act 1991, s100, Schedule 11, para 40(1), (2)(e).

CRIMINAL PROCEDURE (RIGHT OF REPLY) ACT 1964

(1964 c 34)

1 Right of reply at trials on indictment

(1) Upon the trial of any person on indictment –

(a) the prosecution shall not be entitled to the right of reply on the ground only that the Attorney-General of the Solicitor-General appears for the Crown at the trial; and

(b) the time at which the prosecution is entitled to exercise that right shall, notwithstanding anything in section 2 of the Criminal Procedure Act 1865, be after the close of the evidence for the defence and before the closing speech (if any) by or on behalf of the accused.

As amended by the Statute Law (Repeals) Act 1974.

CRIMINAL PROCEDURE (ATTENDANCE OF WITNESSES) ACT 1965

(1965 c 69)

2 Issue of witness summons on application to Crown Court

(1) This section applies where the Crown Court is satisfied that –

(a) a person is likely to be able to give evidence likely to be material evidence, or produce any document or thing likely to be material evidence, for the purpose of any criminal proceedings before the Crown Court, and

(b) the person will not voluntarily attend as a witness or will not voluntarily produce the document or thing.

(2) In such a case the Crown Court shall, subject to the following provisions of this section, issue a summons (a witness summons) directed to the person concerned and requiring him to –

(a) attend before the Crown Court at the time and place stated in the summons, and

(b) give the evidence or produce the document or thing.

(3) A witness summons may only be issued under this section on an application; and the Crown Court may refuse to issue the summons if any requirement relating to the application is not fulfilled.

(4) Where a person has been committed for trial for any offence to which the proceedings concerned relate, an application must be made as soon as is reasonably practicable after the committal.

(5) Where the proceedings concerned have been transferred to the Crown Court, an application must be made as soon as is reasonably practicable after the transfer.

(6) Where the proceedings concerned relate to an offence in relation to which a bill of indictment has been preferred under the authority of section 2(2)(b) of the Administration of Justice (Miscellaneous Provisions) Act 1933 (bill preferred by direction of Court of Appeal, or by direction or with consent of

judge) an application must be made as soon as is reasonably practicable after the bill was preferred.

(7) An application must be made in accordance with Crown Court rules; and different provision may be made for different cases or descriptions of case.

(8) Crown Court rules –

(a) may, in such cases as the rules may specify, require an application to be made by a party to the case;

(b) may, in such cases as the rules may specify, require the service of notice of an application on the person to whom the witness summons is proposed to be directed;

(c) may, in such cases as the rules may specify, require an application to be supported by an affidavit containing such matters as the rules may stipulate;

(d) may, in such cases as the rules may specify, make provision for enabling the person to whom the witness summons is proposed to be directed to be present or represented at the hearing of the application for the witness summons.

(9) Provision contained in Crown Court rules by virtue of subsection (8)(c) above may in particular require an affidavit to –

(a) set out any charge on which the proceedings concerned are based;

(b) specify any stipulated evidence, document or thing in such a way as to enable the directed person to identify it;

(c) specify grounds for believing that the directed person is likely to be able to give any stipulated evidence or produce any stipulated document or thing;

(d) specify grounds for believing that any stipulated evidence is likely to be material evidence;

(e) specify grounds for believing that any stipulated document or thing is likely to be material evidence.

(10) In subsection (9) above –

(a) references to any stipulated evidence, document or thing are to any evidence, document or thing whose giving or production is proposed to be required by the witness summons;

(b) references to the directed person are to the person to whom the witness summons is proposed to be directed.

2A Power to require advance production

A witness summons which is issued under section 2 above and which requires a person to produce a document or thing as mentioned in section 2(2) above may also require him to produce the document or thing –

(a) at a place stated in the summons, and

(b) at a time which is so stated and precedes that stated under section 2(2) above,

for inspection by the person applying for the summons.

2B Summons no longer needed

(1) If –

(a) a document or thing is produced in pursuance of a requirement imposed by a witness summons under section 2A above,

(b) the person applying for the summons concludes that a requirement imposed by the summons under section 2(2) above is no longer needed, and

(c) he accordingly applies to the Crown Court for a direction that the summons shall be of no further effect, the court may direct accordingly.

(2) An application under this section must be made in accordance with Crown Court rules; and different provision may be made for different cases or descriptions of case.

(3) Crown Court rules may, in such cases as the rules may specify, require the effect of a direction under this section to be notified to the person to whom the summons is directed.

2C Application to make summons ineffective

(1) If a witness summons issued under section 2 above is directed to a person who –

(a) applies to the Crown Court,

(b) satisfies the court that he was not served with notice of the application to issue the summons and that he was neither present nor represented at the hearing of the application, and

(c) satisfies the court that he cannot give any evidence likely to be material evidence or, as the case may be, produce any document or thing likely to be material evidence, the court may direct that the summons shall be of no effect.

(2) For the purposes of subsection (1) above it is immaterial –

(a) whether or not Crown Court rules require the person to be served with notice of the application to issue the summons;

(b) whether or not Crown Court rules enable the person to be present or represented at the hearing of the application.

(3) In subsection (1)(b) above 'served' means –

(a) served in accordance with Crown Court rules, in a case where such rules require the person to be served with notice of the application to issue the summons;

(b) served in such way as appears reasonable to the court to which the application is made under this section, in any other case.

(4) The Crown Court may refuse to make a direction under this section if any requirement relating to the application under this section is not fulfilled.

(5) An application under this section must be made in accordance with Crown Court rules; and different provision may be made for different cases or descriptions of case.

(6) Crown Court rules may, in such cases as the rules may specify, require the service of notice of an application under this section on the person on whose application the witness summons was issued.

(7) Crown Court rules may, in such cases as the rules may specify, require that where –

(a) a person applying under this section can produce a particular document or thing, but

(b) he seeks to satisfy the court that the document or thing is not likely to be material evidence,

he must arrange for the document or thing to be available at the hearing of the application.

(8) Where a direction is made under this section that a witness summons shall be of no effect, the person on whose application the summons was issued may be ordered to pay the whole or any part of the costs of the application under this section.

(9) Any costs payable under an order made under subsection (8) above shall be taxed by the proper officer of the court, and payment of those costs shall be enforceable in the same manner as an order for payment of costs made by

the High Court in a civil case or as a sum adjudged summarily to be paid as a civil debt.

2D Issue of witness summons of Crown Court's own motion

For the purpose of any criminal proceedings before it, the Crown Court may of its own motion issue a summons (a witness summons) directed to a person and requiring him to –

(a) attend before the court at the time and place stated in the summons, and

(b) give evidence, or produce any document or thing specified in the summons.

2E Application to make summons ineffective

(1) If a witness summons issued under section 2D above is directed to a person who –

(a) applies to the Crown Court, and

(b) satisfies the court that he cannot give any evidence likely to be material evidence or, as the case may be, produce any document or thing likely to be material evidence,

the court may direct that the summons shall be of no effect.

(2) The Crown Court may refuse to make a direction under this section if any requirement relating to the application under this section is not fulfilled.

(3) An application under this section must be made in accordance with Crown Court rules; and different provision may be made for different cases or descriptions of case.

(4) Crown Court rules may, in such cases as the rules may specify, require that where –

(a) a person applying under this section can produce a particular document or thing, but

(b) he seeks to satisfy the court that the document or thing is not likely to be material evidence,

he must arrange for the document or thing to be available at the hearing of the application.

3 Punishment for disobedience to witness summons

(1) Any person who without just excuse disobeys a witness summons requiring him to attend before any court shall be guilty of contempt of that court and may be punished summarily by that court as if his contempt had been committed in the face of the court.

(1A) Any person who without just excuse disobeys a requirement made by any court under section 2A above shall be guilty of contempt of that court and may be punished summarily by that court as if his contempt had been committed in the face of the court.

(2) No person shall by reason of any disobedience mentioned in subsection (1) or (1A) above be liable to imprisonment for a period exceeding three months.

4 Further process to secure attendance of witness

(1) If a judge of the Crown Court is satisfied by evidence on oath that a witness in respect of whom a witness summons is in force is unlikely to comply with the summons, the judge may issue a warrant to arrest the witness and bring him before the court before which he is required to attend: Provided that a warrant shall not be issued under this subsection unless the judge is satisfied by such evidence as aforesaid that the witness is likely to be able to give evidence likely to be material evidence or produce any document or thing likely to be material evidence in the proceedings.

(2) Where a witness is required to attend before the Crown Court by virtue of a witness summons fails to attend in compliance with the summons, that court may –

(a) in any case, cause to be served on him a notice requiring him to attend the court forthwith or at such time as may be specified in the notice;

(b) if the court is satisfied that there are reasonable grounds for believing that he has failed to attend without just excuse, or if he has failed to comply with a notice under paragraph (a) above, issue a warrant to arrest him and bring him before the court.

(3) A witness brought before the court in pursuance of a warrant under this section may be remanded by that court in custody or on bail (with or without sureties) until such time as the court may appoint for receiving his evidence or dealing with him under section 3 of this Act; and where a witness attends a court in pursuance of a notice under this section the court may direct that the notice shall have effect as if it required him to attend

at any later time appointed by the court for receiving his evidence or dealing with him as aforesaid.

8 Abolition of subpoenas in certain proceedings

No subpoena ad testificandum or subpoena duces tecum shall issue after the commencement of this Act in respect of any proceedings for the purpose of which a witness summons may be issued under section 2 of this Act or in respect of any proceedings for the purpose of which a summons may be issued under section 97 of the Magistrates' Courts Act 1980 (process for attendance of witnesses in magistrates' courts).

As amended by the Courts Act 1971, s56(1), Schedule 8, Pt II, para 45(4); Magistrates' Courts Act 1980, s154, Schedule 7, para 56; Criminal Procedure and Investigations Act 1996, ss65(1), 66, 67(1), 80, Schedule 5(6), s67(1) from a day to be appointed.

CRIMINAL JUSTICE ACT 1967
(1967 c 80)

8 Proof of criminal intent

A court or jury, in determining whether a person has committed an offence, –

(a) shall not be bound in law to infer that he intended or foresaw a result of the actions by reason only of its being a natural and probable consequence of those actions; but

(b) shall decide whether he did intend or foresee that result by reference to all the evidence, drawing such inferences from the evidence as appear proper in the circumstances.

9 Proof by written statement

(1) In any criminal proceedings, other than committal proceedings, a written statement by any person shall, if such of the conditions mentioned in the next following subsection as are applicable are satisfied, be admissible as evidence to the like extent as oral evidence to the like effect by that person.

(2) The said conditions are –

(a) the statement purports to be signed by the person who made it;

(b) the statement contains a declaration by that person to the effect that it is true to the best of his knowledge and belief and that he made the statement knowing that, if it were tendered in evidence, he would be liable to prosecution if he wilfully stated in it anything which he knew to be false or did not believe to be true;

(c) before the hearing at which the statement is tendered in evidence, a copy of the statement is served, by or on behalf of the party proposing to tender it, on each of the other parties to the proceedings; and

(d) none of the other parties or their solicitors, within seven days from the service of the copy of the statement, serves a notice on the party so proposing objecting to the statement being tendered in evidence under this section:

Provided that the conditions mentioned in paragraphs (c) and (d) of this subsection shall not apply if the parties agree before or during the hearing that the statement shall be so tendered.

(3) The following provisions shall also have effect in relation to any written statement tendered in evidence under this section, that is to say –

(a) if the statement is made by a person under the age of eighteen, it shall give his age;

(b) if it is made by a person who cannot read it, it shall be read to him before he signs it and shall be accompanied by a declaration by the person who so read the statement to the effect that it was so read; and

(c) if it refers to any other document as an exhibit, the copy served on any other party to the proceedings under paragraph (c) of the last foregoing subsection shall be accompanied by a copy of that document or by such information as may be necessary in order to enable the party on whom it is served to inspect that document or a copy thereof.

(4) Notwithstanding that a written statement made by any person may be admissible as evidence by virtue of this section –

(a) the party by whom or on whose behalf a copy of the statement was served may call that person to give evidence; and

(b) the court may, of its own motion or on the application of any party to the proceedings, require that person to attend before the court and give evidence.

(5) An application under paragraph (b) of the last foregoing subsection to a court other than a magistrates' court may be made before the hearing and on any such application the powers of the court shall be exercisable by a puisne judge of the High Court, a circuit judge or recorder sitting alone.

(6) So much of any statement as is admitted in evidence by virtue of this section shall, unless the court otherwise directs, be read aloud at the hearing and where the court so directs an account shall be given orally of so much of any statement as is not read aloud.

(7) Any document or object referred to as an exhibit and identified in a written statement tendered in evidence under this section shall be treated as if it had been produced as an exhibit and identified in court by the maker of the statement.

(8) A document required by this section to be served on any person may be served –

(a) by delivering it to him or to his solicitor; or

(b) by addressing it to him and leaving it at his usual or last known place of abode or place of business or by addressing it to his solicitor and leaving it at his office; or

(c) by sending it in a registered letter or by the recorded delivery service or by first class post addressed to him at his usual or last known place of abode or place of business or addressed to his solicitor at his office; or

(d) in the case of a body corporate, by delivering it to the secretary or clerk of the body at its registered or principal office or sending it in a registered letter or by the recorded delivery service or by first class post addressed to the secretary or clerk of that body at that office.

10 Proof by formal admission

(1) Subject to the provisions of this section, any fact of which oral evidence may be given in any criminal proceedings may be admitted for the purpose of those proceedings by or on behalf of the prosecutor or defendant, and the admission by any party of any such fact under this section shall as against that party be conclusive evidence in those proceedings of the fact admitted.

(2) An admission under this section –

(a) may be made before or at the proceedings;

(b) if made otherwise than in court, shall be in writing;

(c) if made in writing by an individual, shall purport to be signed by the person making it and, if so made by a body corporate, shall purport to be signed by a director or manager, or the secretary or clerk, or some other similar officer of the body corporate;

(d) if made on behalf of a defendant who is an individual, shall be made by his counsel or solicitor;

(e) if made at any stage before the trial by a defendant who is an individual, must be approved by his counsel or solicitor (whether at the time it was made or subsequently) before or at the proceedings in question.

(3) An admission under this section for the purpose of proceedings relating to any matter shall be treated as an admission for the purpose of any subsequent criminal proceedings relating to that matter (including any appeal or retrial).

(4) An admission under this section may with the leave of the court be withdrawn in the proceedings for the purpose of which it is made or any subsequent criminal proceedings relating to the same matter.

As amended by the Courts Act 1971, s56(1), Schedule 8, Pt II, para 49; Magistrates' Courts Act 1980, s154, Schedule 7, paras 63, 64; Criminal Justice Act 1987, s15, Schedule 2, para 2; Criminal Justice and Public Order Act 1994, s168(1), Schedule 9, para 6; Criminal Procedure and Investigations Act 1996, ss69, 74(1), (5), 80, Schedule 5(9).

THEFT ACT 1968

(1968 c 60)

27 Evidence and procedure on charge of theft or handling stolen goods

(3) Where a person is being proceeded against for handling stolen goods (but not for any offence other than handling stolen goods), then at any stage of the proceedings, if evidence has been given of his having or arranging to have in his possession the goods the subject of the charge, or of his undertaking or assisting in, or arranging to undertake or assist in, their retention, removal, disposal or realisation, the following evidence shall be admissible for the purpose of proving that he knew or believed the goods to be stolen goods –

(a) evidence that he has had in his possession, or has undertaken or assisted in the retention, removal, disposal or realisation of, stolen goods from any theft taking place not earlier than twelve months before the offence charged; and

(b) (provided that seven days' notice in writing has been given to him of the intention to prove the conviction) evidence that he has within the five years preceding the date of the offence charged been convicted of theft or of handling stolen goods.

(4) In any proceedings for the theft of anything in the course of transmission (whether by post or otherwise), or for handling stolen goods from such a theft, a statutory declaration made by any person that he despatched or received or failed to receive any goods or postal packet, or that any goods or postal packet when despatched or received by him were in a particular state or condition, shall be admissible as evidence of the facts stated in the declaration, subject to the following conditions –

(a) a statutory declaration shall only be admissible where and to the extent to which oral evidence to the like effect would have been admissible in the proceedings; and

(b) a statutory declaration shall only be admissible if at least seven days before the hearing or trial a copy of it has been given to the person charged, and he has not, at least three days before the hearing or trial or within such further time as the court may in special circumstances allow, given the prosecutor written notice requiring the attendance at the hearing or trial of the person making the declaration.

(4A) Where the proceedings mentioned in subsection (4) above are proceedings before a magistrates' court inquiring into an offence as examining justices that subsection shall have effect with the omission of the words from 'subject to the following conditions' to the end of the subsection.

30 Husband and wife

(1) This Act shall apply in relation to the parties to a marriage, and to property belonging to the wife or husband whether or not by reason of an interest derived from the marriage, as it would apply if they were not married and any such interest subsisted independently of the marriage.

(2) Subject to subsection (4) below, a person shall have the same right to bring proceedings against that person's wife or husband for any offence (whether under this Act or otherwise) as if they were not married, and a person bringing any such proceedings shall be competent to give evidence for the prosecution at every stage of the proceedings.

(4) Proceedings shall not be instituted against a person for any offence of stealing or doing unlawful damage to property which at the time of the offence belongs to that person's wife or husband, or for any attempt, incitement or conspiracy to commit such an offence, unless the proceedings are instituted by or with the consent of the Director of Public Prosecutions:

Provided that –

(a) this subsection shall not apply to proceedings against a person for an offence –

(i) if that person is charged with committing the offence jointly with the wife or husband; or

(ii) if by virtue of any judicial decree or order (wherever made) that person and the wife or husband are at the time of the offence under no obligation to cohabit.

31 Effect on civil proceedings and rights

(1) A person shall not be excused, by reason that to do so may incriminate that person or the wife or husband of that person of an offence under this Act –

(a) from answering any question put to that person in proceedings for the recovery or administration of any property, for the execution of any trust or for an account of any property or dealings with property; or

(b) from complying with any order made in any such proceedings;

but no statement or admission made by a person in answering a question put or complying with an order made as aforesaid shall, in proceedings for an offence under this Act, be admissible in evidence against that person or (unless they married after the making of the statement or admission) against the wife or husband of that person.

As amended by the Criminal Procedure and Investigations Act 1996, s47, Schedule 1, Pt II, para 19.

CIVIL EVIDENCE ACT 1968
(1968 c 64)

PART II

MISCELLANEOUS AND GENERAL

11 Convictions as evidence in civil proceedings

(1) In any civil proceedings the fact that a person has been convicted of an offence by or before any court in the United Kingdom or by a court-martial there or elsewhere shall (subject to subsection (3) below) be admissible in evidence for the purpose of proving, where to do so is relevant to any issue in those proceedings, that he committed that offence, whether he was so convicted upon a plea of guilty or otherwise and whether or not he is a party to the civil proceedings; but no conviction other than a subsisting one shall be admissible in evidence by virtue of this section.

(2) In any civil proceedings in which by virtue of this section a person is proved to have been convicted of an offence by or before any court in the United Kingdom or by a court-martial there or elsewhere –

(a) he shall be taken to have committed that offence unless the contrary is proved; and

(b) without prejudice to the reception of any other admissible evidence for the purpose of identifying the facts on which the conviction was based, the contents of any document which is admissible as evidence of the conviction, and the contents of the information, complaint, indictment or charge-sheet on which the person in question was convicted, shall be admissible in evidence for that purpose.

(3) Nothing in this section shall prejudice the operation of section 13 of this Act or any other enactment whereby a conviction or a finding of fact in any criminal proceedings is for the purposes of any other proceedings made conclusive evidence of any fact.

(4) Where in any civil proceedings the contents of any document are admissible in evidence by virtue of subsection (2) above, a copy of that document, or of the material part thereof, purporting to be certified or

otherwise authenticated by or on behalf of the court or authority having custody of that document shall be admissible in evidence and shall be taken to be a true copy of that document or part unless the contrary is shown.

(5) Nothing in any of the following enactments, that is to say –

(a) section 1C of the Powers of Criminal Courts Act 1973 (under which a conviction leading to discharge is to be disregarded except as therein mentioned); ...

shall affect the operation of this section; ...

(6) In this section 'court-martial' means a court-martial constituted under the Army Act 1955, the Air Force Act 1955 or the Naval Discipline Act 1957 or a disciplinary court constituted under section 50 of the said Act of 1957, and in relation to a court-martial 'conviction', as regards court-martial constituted under either of the said Acts of 1955, means a finding of guilty which is, or falls to be treated as, a finding of the court duly confirmed and, as regards a court-martial or disciplinary court constituted under the said Act of 1957, means a finding of guilty which is, or falls to be treated as, the finding of the court, and 'convicted' shall be construed accordingly.

12 Findings of adultery and paternity as evidence in civil proceedings

(1) In any civil proceedings –

(a) the fact that a person has been found guilty of adultery in any matrimonial proceedings; and

(b) the fact that a person has been found to be the father of a child in relevant proceedings before any court in England and Wales ... or has been adjudged to be the father of a child in affiliation proceedings before any court in the United Kingdom;

shall (subject to subsection (3) below) be admissible in evidence for the purpose of proving, where to do so is relevant to any issue in those civil proceedings, that he committed the adultery to which the finding relates or, as the case may be, is (or was) the father of that child, whether or not he offered any defence to the allegation of adultery or paternity and whether or not he is a party to the civil proceedings; but no finding or adjudication other than a subsisting one shall be admissible in evidence by virtue of this section.

(2) In any civil proceedings in which by virtue of this section a person is proved to have been found guilty of adultery as mentioned in subsection (1)(a) above or to have been found or adjudged to be the father of a child as mentioned in subsection (1)(b) above –

(a) he shall be taken to have committed the adultery to which the finding relates or, as the case may be, to be (or have been) the father of that child, unless the contrary is proved; and

(b) without prejudice to the reception of any other admissible evidence for the purpose of identifying the facts on which the finding or adjudication was based, the contents of any document which was before the court, or which contains any pronouncement of the court, in the other proceedings in question shall be admissible in evidence for that purpose.

(3) Nothing in this section shall prejudice the operation of any enactment whereby a finding of fact in any matrimonial or affiliation proceedings is for the purposes of any other proceedings made conclusive evidence of any fact.

(4) Subsection (4) of section 11 of this Act shall apply for the purposes of this section as if the reference to subsection (2) were a reference to subsection (2) of this section.

(5) In this section –

'matrimonial proceedings' means any matrimonial cause in the High Court or a county court in England and Wales or in the High Court in Northern Ireland, any consistorial action in Scotland, or any appeal arising out of any such cause or action;

'relevant proceedings' means –

(a) proceedings on a complaint under section 42 of the National Assistance Act 1948 or section 26 of the Social Security Act 1986;

(b) proceedings under the Children Act 1989;

(c) proceedings which would have been relevant proceedings for the purposes of this section in the form in which it was in force before the passing of the Children Act 1989 ...

(d) section 27 of the Child Support Act 1991. ...

13 Conclusiveness of convictions for purposes of defamation actions

(1) In an action for libel or slander in which the question whether the plaintiff did or did not commit a criminal offence is relevant to an issue arising in the action, proof that at the time when that issue falls to be determined, he stands convicted of that offence shall be conclusive evidence that he committed that offence; and his conviction thereof shall be admissible in evidence accordingly.

(2) In any such action as aforesaid in which by virtue of this section the plaintiff is proved to have been convicted of an offence, the contents of any document which is admissible as evidence of the conviction, and the contents of the information, complaint, indictment or charge-sheet on which he was convicted, shall, without prejudice to the reception of any other admissible evidence for the purpose of identifying the facts on which the conviction was based, be admissible in evidence for the purpose of identifying those facts.

(2A) In the case of an action for libel or slander in which there is more than one plaintiff –

(a) the references in subsections (1) and (2) above to the plaintiff shall be construed as references to any of the plaintiffs, and

(b) proof that any of the plaintiffs stands convicted of an offence shall be conclusive evidence that he committed that offence so far as that fact is relevant to any issue arising in relation to his cause of action or that of any other plaintiff.

(3) For the purposes of this section a person shall be taken to stand convicted of an offence if but only if there subsists against him a conviction of that offence by or before a court in the United Kingdom or by a court-martial there or elsewhere.

(4) Subsections (4) to (6) of section 11 of this Act shall apply for the purposes of this section as they apply for the purposes of that section, but as if in the said subsection (4) the reference to subsection (2) was a reference to subsection (2) of this section.

(5) The foregoing provisions of this section shall apply for the purposes of any action begun after the passing of this Act, whenever the cause of action arose, but shall not apply for the purposes of any action begun before the passing of this Act or any appeal or other proceedings arising out of any such action.

14 Privilege against incrimination of self or spouse

(1) The right of a person in any legal proceedings other than criminal proceedings to refuse to answer any question or produce any document or thing if to do so would tend to expose that person to proceedings for an offence or for the recovery of a penalty –

(a) shall apply only as regards criminal offences under the law of any part of the United Kingdom and penalties provided for by such law; and

(b) shall include a like right to refuse to answer any question or produce any document or thing if to do so would tend to expose the husband or wife of that person to proceedings for any such criminal offence or for the recovery of any such penalty.

(2) In so far as any existing enactment conferring (in whatever words) powers of inspection or investigation confers on a person (in whatever words) any right otherwise than in criminal proceedings to refuse to answer any question or give any evidence tending to incriminate that person, subsection (1) above shall apply to that right as it applies to the right described in that subsection; and every such existing enactment shall be construed accordingly.

(3) In so far as any existing enactment provides (in whatever words) that in any proceedings other than criminal proceedings a person shall not be excused from answering any question or giving any evidence on the ground that to do so may incriminate that person, that enactment shall be construed as providing also that in such proceedings a person shall not be excused from answering any question or giving any evidence on the ground that to do so may incriminate the husband or wife of that person.

(4) Where any existing enactment (however worded) that –

(a) confers powers of inspection or investigation; or

(b) provides as mentioned in subsection (3) above,

further provides (in whatever words) that any answer or evidence given by a person shall be admissible in evidence against that person in any proceedings or class of proceedings (however described, and whether criminal or not), that enactment shall be construed as providing also that any answer or evidence given by that person shall not be admissible in evidence against the husband and wife of that person in the proceedings or class of proceedings in question.

(5) In this section 'existing enactment' means any enactment passed before this Act; and the references to giving evidence are references to giving evidence in any manner, whether by furnishing information, making discovery, producing documents or otherwise.

16 Abolition of certain privileges

(1) The following rules of law are hereby abrogated except in relation to criminal proceedings, that is to say –

(a) the rule whereby, in any legal proceedings, a person cannot be compelled to answer any question or produce any document or thing if to do so would tend to expose him to a forfeiture; and

(b) the rule whereby, in any legal proceedings, a person other than a party to the proceedings cannot be compelled to produce any deed or other document relating to his title to any land.

(2) The rule of law whereby, in any civil proceedings, a party to the proceedings cannot be compelled to produce any document relating solely to his own case and in no way tending to impeach that case or support the case of any opposing party is hereby abrogated.

(3) Section 3 of the Evidence (Amendment) Act 1853 (which provides that a husband or wife shall not be compellable to disclose any communication made to him or her by his or her spouse during the marriage) shall cease to have effect except in relation to criminal proceedings.

(5) A witness in any proceedings instituted in consequence of adultery, whether a party to the proceedings or not, shall not be excused from answering any question by reason that it tends to show that he or she has been guilty of adultery.

17 Consequential amendments relating to privilege

(1) In relation to England and Wales –

(a) section 1(3) of the Tribunals of Inquiry (Evidence) Act 1921 (under which a witness before a tribunal to which that Act has been applied is entitled to the same privileges as if he were a witness before the High Court) shall have effect as if after the word 'witness', in the second place where it occurs, there were inserted the words 'in civil proceedings'; and

(b) section 8(5) of the Parliamentary Commissioner Act 1967 (which provides that, subject as there mentioned, no person shall be compelled for the purposes of an investigation under that Act to give any evidence or produce any document which he could not be compelled to give or produce in proceedings before the High Court) shall have effect as if before the word 'proceedings' there were inserted the word 'civil';

and, so far as it applies to England and Wales, any other existing enactment, however framed or worded, which in relation to any tribunal, investigation or inquiry (however described) confers on persons required to answer questions or give evidence any privilege described by reference to the privileges of witnesses in proceedings before any court shall, unless the contrary intention appears, be construed as referring to the privileges of witnesses in civil proceedings before that court.

(3) Without prejudice to the generality of subsections (2) to (4) of section 14 of this Act, the enactments mentioned in the Schedule to this Act shall

have effect subject to the amendments provided for by that Schedule (being verbal amendments to bring those enactments into conformity with the provisions of that section).

(4) Subsection (5) of section 14 of this Act shall apply for the purposes of this section as it applies for the purposes of that section.

18 General interpretation and savings

(1) In this Act 'civil proceedings' includes, in addition to civil proceedings in any of the ordinary courts of law –

(a) civil proceedings before any other tribunal, being proceedings in relation to which the strict rules of evidence apply; and

(b) an arbitration or reference, whether under an enactment or not,

but does not include civil proceedings in relation to which the strict rules of evidence do not apply.

(2) In this Act –

'court' does not include a court-martial, and, in relation to an arbitration or reference, means the arbitrator or umpire and, in relation to proceedings before a tribunal (not being one of the ordinary courts of law), means the tribunal;

'legal proceedings' includes an arbitration or reference, whether under an enactment or not;

and for the avoidance of doubt it is hereby declared that in this Act, and in any amendment made by this Act in any other enactment, references to a person's husband or wife do not include references to a person who is no longer married to that person.

(3) Any reference in this Act to any other enactment is a reference thereto as amended, and includes a reference thereto as applied, by or under any other enactment.

(4) Nothing in this Act shall prejudice the operation of any enactment which provides (in whatever words) that any answer or evidence given by a person in specified circumstances shall not be admissible in evidence against him or some other person in any proceedings or class of proceedings (however described).

In this subsection the reference to giving evidence is a reference to giving evidence in any manner, whether by furnishing information, making discovery, producing documents or otherwise.

(5) Nothing in this Act shall prejudice –

(a) any power of a court, in any legal proceedings, to exclude evidence (whether by preventing questions from being put or otherwise) at its discretion; or

(b) the operation of any agreement (whenever made) between the parties to any legal proceedings as to the evidence which is to be admissible (whether generally or for any particular purpose) in those proceedings.

(6) It is hereby declared that where, by reason of any defect of speech or hearing from which he is suffering, a person called as a witness in any legal proceedings gives his evidence in writing or by signs, that evidence is to be treated for the purposes of this Act as being given orally.

As amended by the Powers of Criminal Courts Act 1973, ss56(1), 60(2), Schedule 5, para 31; Family Law Reform Act 1987, s29(1)-(3); Courts and Legal Services Act 1990, s116, Schedule 16, para 2(1); Criminal Justice Act 1991, ss100, 101(2), Schedule 11, para 5, Schedule 13; Defamation Act 1996, s12(1).

FAMILY LAW REFORM ACT 1969

(1969 c 46)

20 Power of court to require use of blood tests

(1) In any civil proceedings in which the paternity of any person falls to be determined by the court hearing the proceedings, the court may, on an application by any party to the proceedings, give a direction for the use of blood tests to ascertain whether such tests show that a party to the proceedings is or is not thereby excluded from being the father of that person and for the taking, within a period to be specified in the direction, of blood samples from that person, the mother of that person and any party alleged to be the father of that person or from any, or any two, of those persons.

A court may at any time revoke or vary a direction previously given by it under this section.

(1A) Where –

(a) an application is made for a direction under this section; and

(b) the person whose paternity is in issue is under the age of eighteen when the application is made,

the application shall specify who is to carry out the tests.

(1B) In the case of a direction made on an application to which subsection (1A) applies the court shall –

(a) specify, as the person who is to carry out the tests, the person specified in the application; or

(b) where the court considers that it would be inappropriate to specify that person (whether because to specify him would be incompatible with any provision made by or under regulations made under section 22 of this Act or for any other reason), decline to give the direction applied for.

(2) The person responsible for carrying out blood tests taken for the purposes of giving effect to a direction under this section shall make to the court by which the direction was given a report in which he shall state –

(a) the results of the tests;

(b) whether the party to whom the report relates is or is not excluded by the results from being the father of the person whose paternity is to be determined; and

(c) if that party is not so excluded, the value, if any, of the results in determining whether that party is that person's father;

and the report shall be received by the court as evidence in the proceedings of the matters stated therein.

(3) A report under subsection (2) of this section shall be in the form prescribed by regulations made under section 22 of this Act.

(4) Where a report has been made to a court under subsection (2) of this section, any party may, with the leave of the court, or shall, if the court so directs, obtain from the person who made the report a written statement explaining or amplifying any statement made in the report, and that statement shall be deemed for the purposes of this section (except subsection (3) thereof) to form part of the report made to the court.

(5) Where a direction is given under this section in any proceedings, a party to the proceedings, unless the court otherwise directs, shall not be entitled to call as a witness the person responsible for carrying out the tests taken for the purpose of giving effect to the direction, or any person by whom any thing necessary for the purpose of enabling those tests to be carried out was done, unless within fourteen days after receiving a copy of the report he serves notice on the other parties to the proceedings, or on such of them as the court may direct, of his intention to call that person; and where any such person is called as a witness the party who called him shall be entitled to cross-examine him.

(6) Where a direction is given under this section the party on whose application the direction is given shall pay the cost of taking and testing blood samples for the purpose of giving effect to the direction (including any expenses reasonably incurred by any person in taking any steps required of him for the purpose), and of making a report to the court under this section, but the amount paid shall be treated as costs incurred by him in the proceedings.

26 Rebuttal of presumption as to legitimacy and illegitimacy

Any presumption of law as to the legitimacy or illegitimacy of any person may in any civil proceedings be rebutted by evidence which shows that it is more probable than not that that person is illegitimate or legitimate, as the case may be, and it shall not be necessary to prove that fact beyond reasonable doubt in order to rebut the presumption.

NB As from a day yet to be appointed, s20(1), (2) have been substituted, and s20(6) has been amended, by the Family Law Reform Act 1987, ss23(1), 33(1), Schedule 2, para 21.

As amended by the Children Act 1989, s89; Courts and Legal Services Act 1990, s116, Schedule 16, Pt I, para 3.

CRIMINAL DAMAGE ACT 1971

(1971 c 48)

9 Evidence in connection with offences under this Act

A person shall not be excused, by reason that to do so may incriminate that person or the wife or husband of that person of an offence under this Act –

(a) from answering any question put to that person in proceedings for the recovery or administration of any property, for the execution of any trust or for an account of any property or dealings with property; or

(b) from complying with any order made in any such proceedings;

but no statement or admission made by a person in answering a question put or complying with an order made as aforesaid shall, in proceedings for an offence under this Act, be admissible in evidence against that person or (unless they married after the making of the statement or admission) against the wife or husband of that person.

CIVIL EVIDENCE ACT 1972
(1972 c 30)

2 Rules of court with respect to expert reports and oral expert evidence

(3) Notwithstanding any enactment or rule of law by virtue of which documents prepared for the purpose of pending or contemplated civil proceedings or in connection with the obtaining or giving of legal advice are in certain circumstances privileged from disclosure, provision may be made by rules of court –

(a) for enabling the court in any civil proceedings to direct, with respect to medical matters or matters of any other class which may be specified in the direction, that the parties or some of them shall each by such date as may be so specified (or such later date as may be permitted or agreed in accordance with the rules) disclose to the other or others in the form of one or more expert reports the expert evidence on matters of that class which he proposes to adduce as part of his case at the trial; and

(b) for prohibiting a party who fails to comply with a direction given in any such proceedings under rules of court made by virtue of paragraph (a) above from adducing in evidence, except with the leave of the court, any statement (whether of fact or opinion) contained in any expert report whatsoever in so far as that statement deals with matters of any class specified in the direction.

(4) Provision may be made by rules of court as to the conditions subject to which oral expert evidence may be given in civil proceedings.

(5) Without prejudice to the generality of subsection (4) above, rules of court made in pursuance of that subsection may make provision for prohibiting a party who fails to comply with a direction given as mentioned in subsection (3)(b) above from adducing, except with the leave of the court, any oral expert evidence whatsoever with respect to matters of any class specified in the direction.

(6) Any rules of court made in pursuance of this section may make different provision for different classes of cases, for expert reports dealing with matters of different classes, and for other different circumstances.

(7) References in this section to an expert report are references to a written report by a person dealing wholly or mainly with matters on which he is (or would if living be) qualified to give expert evidence.

(8) Nothing in the foregoing provisions of this section shall prejudice the generality of section 75 of the County Courts Act 1984, section 144 of the Magistrates' Courts Act 1980 or any other enactment conferring power to make rules of court; and nothing in section 75(2) of the County Courts Act 1984 or any other enactment restricting the matters with respect to which rules of court may be made shall prejudice the making of rules of court in pursuance of this section or the operation of any rules of court so made.

3 Admissibility of expert opinion and certain expressions of non-expert opinion

(1) Subject to any rules of court made in pursuance of this Act, where a person is called as a witness in any civil proceedings, his opinion on any relevant matter on which he is qualified to give expert evidence shall be admissible in evidence.

(2) It is hereby declared that where a person is called as a witness in any civil proceedings, a statement of opinion by him on any relevant matter on which he is not qualified to give expert evidence, if made as a way of conveying relevant facts personally perceived by him, is admissible as evidence of what he perceived.

(3) In this section 'relevant matter' includes an issue in the proceedings in question.

4 Evidence of foreign law

(1) It is hereby declared that in civil proceedings a person who is suitably qualified to do so on account of his knowledge or experience is competent to give expert evidence as to the law of any country or territory outside the United Kingdom, or of any part of the United Kingdom other than England and Wales, irrespective of whether he has acted or is entitled to act as a legal practitioner there.

(2) Where any question as to the law of any country or territory outside the United Kingdom, or of any part of the United Kingdom other than England and Wales, with respect to any matter has been determined (whether before or after the passing of this Act) in any such proceedings as are mentioned in subsection (4) below, then in any civil proceedings (not being proceedings before a court which can take judicial notice of the law of that country, territory or part with respect to that matter) –

(a) any finding made or decision given on that question in the first-mentioned proceedings shall, if reported or recorded in citable form, be admissible in evidence for the purpose of proving the law of that country, territory or part with respect to that matter; and

(b) if that finding or decision, as so reported or recorded, is adduced for that purpose, the law of that country, territory or part with respect to that matter shall be taken to be in accordance with that finding or decision unless the contrary is proved:

Provided that paragraph (b) above shall not apply in the case of a finding or decision which conflicts with another finding or decision on the same question adduced by virtue of this subsection in the same proceedings.

(3) Except with the leave of the court, a party to any civil proceedings shall not be permitted to adduce any such finding or decision as is mentioned in subsection (2) above by virtue of that subsection unless he has in accordance with rules of court given to every other party to the proceedings notice that he intends to do so.

(4) The proceedings referred to in subsection (2) above are the following, whether civil or criminal, namely –

(a) proceedings at first instance in any of the following courts, namely the High Court, the Crown Court, a court of quarter sessions, the Court of Chancery of the county palatine of Lancaster and the Court of Chancery of the county palatine of Durham;

(b) appeals arising out of any such proceedings as are mentioned in paragraph (a) above;

(c) proceedings before the Judicial Committee of the Privy Council on appeal (whether to Her Majesty in Council or to the Judicial Committee as such) from any decision of any court outside the United Kingdom.

(5) For the purposes of this section a finding or decision on any such question as is mentioned in subsection (2) above shall be taken to be reported or recorded in citable form, if, but only if, it is reported or recorded in writing in a report, transcript or other document which, if that question had been a question as to the law of England and Wales, could be cited as an authority in legal proceedings in England and Wales.

5 Interpretation, application to arbitrations, etc and savings

(1) In this Act 'civil proceedings' means civil proceedings, before any tribunal, in relation to which the strict rules of evidence apply, whether as a matter of law or by agreement of the parties; and references to 'the court' shall be construed accordingly.

(2) The rules of court made for the purposes of the application of sections 2 and 4 of this Act to proceedings in the High Court apply, except in so far as their application is excluded by agreement, to proceedings before tribunals other than the ordinary courts of law, subject to such modifications as may be appropriate. Any question arising as to what modifications are appropriate shall be determined, in default of agreement, by the tribunal.

(3) Nothing in this Act shall prejudice –

(a) any power of a court, in any civil proceedings, to exclude evidence (whether by preventing questions from being put or otherwise) at its discretion; or

(b) the operation of any agreement (whenever made) between the parties to any civil proceedings as to the evidence which is to be admissible (whether generally or for any particular purpose) in those proceedings.

As amended by the Civil Evidence Act 1995, s15(1), (2), Schedule 1, para 7, Schedule 2.

MATRIMONIAL CAUSES ACT 1973

(1973 c 18)

19 Presumption of death and dissolution of marriage

(1) Any married person who alleges that reasonable grounds exist for supposing that the other party to the marriage is dead may present a petition to the court to have it presumed that the other party is dead and to have the marriage dissolved, and the court may, if satisfied that such reasonable grounds exist, grant a decree of presumption of death and dissolution of the marriage.

(3) In any proceedings under this section the fact that for a period of seven years or more the other party to the marriage has been continually absent from the petitioner and the petitioner has no reason to believe that the other party has been living within that time shall be evidence that the other party is dead until the contrary is proved.

48 Evidence

(1) The evidence of a husband or wife shall be admissible in any proceedings to prove that marital intercourse did or did not take place between them during any period.

(2) In any proceedings for nullity of marriage, evidence on the question of sexual capacity shall be heard in camera unless in any case the judge is satisfied that in the interests of justice any such evidence ought to be heard in open court.

As amended by the Domicile and Matrimonial Proceedings Act 1973, s17(2), Schedule 6.

REHABILITATION OF OFFENDERS ACT 1974

(1974 c 53)

4 Effect of rehabilitation

(1) Subject to sections 7 and 8 below, a person who has become a rehabilitated person for the purposes of this Act in respect of a conviction shall be treated for all purposes in law as a person who has not committed or been charged with or prosecuted for or convicted of or sentenced for the offence or offences which were the subject of that conviction; and, notwithstanding the provisions of any other enactment or rule of law to the contrary, but subject as aforesaid –

(a) no evidence shall be admissible in any proceedings before a judicial authority exercising its jurisdiction or functions in Great Britain to prove that any such person has committed or been charged with or prosecuted for or convicted of or sentenced for any offence which was the subject of a spent conviction; and

(b) a person shall not, in any such proceedings, be asked, and, if asked, shall not be required to answer, any question relating to his past which cannot be answered without acknowledging or referring to a spent conviction or spent convictions or any circumstances ancillary thereto.

(2) Subject to the provisions of any order made under subsection (4) below, where a question seeking information with respect to a person's previous convictions, offences, conduct or circumstances is put to him or to any other person otherwise than in proceedings before a judicial authority –

(a) the question shall be treated as not relating to spent convictions or to any circumstances ancillary to spent convictions, and the answer thereto may be framed accordingly, and

(b) the person questioned shall not be subjected to any liability or otherwise prejudiced in law by reason of any failure to acknowledge or disclose a spent conviction or any circumstances ancillary to a spent conviction in his answer to the question.

(3) Subject to the provisions of any order made under subsection (4) below –

(a) any obligation imposed on any person by any rule of law or by the provisions of any agreement or arrangement to disclose any matters to any other person shall not extend to requiring him to disclose a spent conviction or any circumstances ancillary to a spent conviction (whether the conviction is his own or another's); and

(b) a conviction which has become spent or any circumstances ancillary thereto, or any failure to disclose a spent conviction or any such circumstances, shall not be a proper ground for dismissing or excluding a person from any office, profession, occupation or employment, or for prejudicing him in any way in any occupation or employment.

(4) The Secretary of State may by order –

(a) make such provisions as seems to him appropriate for excluding or modifying the application of either or both of paragraphs (a) and (b) of subsection (2) above in relation to questions put in such circumstances as may be specified in the order;

(b) provide for such exceptions from the provisions of subsection (3) above as seem to him appropriate, in such cases or classes of case, and in relation to convictions of such a description, as may be specified in the order.

(5) For the purposes of this section and section 7 below any of the following are circumstances ancillary to a conviction, that is to say –

(a) the offence or offences which were the subject of that conviction;

(b) the conduct constituting that offence or those offences; and

(c) any process or proceedings preliminary to that conviction, any sentence imposed in respect of that conviction, any proceedings (whether by way of appeal or otherwise) for reviewing that conviction or any such sentence, and anything done in pursuance of or undergone in compliance with any such sentence.

(6) For the purposes of this section and section 7 below 'proceedings before a judicial authority' includes, in addition to proceedings before any of the ordinary courts of law, proceedings before any tribunal, body or person having power –

(a) by virtue of any enactment, law, custom or practice;

(b) under the rules governing any association, institution, profession, occupation or employment; or

(c) under any provision of an agreement providing for arbitration with respect to questions arising thereunder;

to determine any question affecting the rights, privileges, obligations or liabilities of any person, or to receive evidence affecting the determination of any such question.

7 Limitations on rehabilitation under this Act, etc

(1) Nothing in section 4(1) above shall affect –

(a) any right of Her Majesty, by virtue of Her Royal prerogative or otherwise, to grant a free pardon, to quash any conviction or sentence, or to commute any sentence;

(b) the enforcement by any process or proceedings of any fine or other sum adjudged to be paid by or imposed on a spent conviction;

(c) the issue of any process for the purpose of proceedings in respect of any breach of a condition or requirement applicable to a sentence imposed in respect of a spent conviction; or

(d) the operation of any enactment by virtue of which, in consequence of any conviction, a person is subject, otherwise than by way of sentence, to any disqualification, disability, prohibition or other penalty the period of which extends beyond the rehabilitation period applicable in accordance with section 6 above to the conviction.

(2) Nothing in section 4(1) above shall affect the determination of any issue, or prevent the admission or requirement of any evidence, relating to a person's previous convictions or to circumstances ancillary thereto –

(a) in any criminal proceedings before a court in Great Britain (including any appeal or reference in a criminal matter);

(b) in any service disciplinary proceedings or in any proceedings on appeal from any service disciplinary proceedings;

(c) in any proceedings relating to adoption, the marriage of any minor, the exercise of the inherent jurisdiction of the High Court with respect to minors or the provision by any person of accommodation, care or schooling for minors;

(cc) in any proceedings brought under the Children Act 1989;

(d) in any proceedings relating to the variation or discharge of a supervision order under the Children and Young Persons Act 1969, or an appeal from any such proceedings ...

(f) in any proceedings in which he is a party or a witness, provided that, on the occasion when the issue or the admission or requirement of the evidence falls to be determined, he consents to the determination of the issue or, as the case may be, the admission or requirement of the evidence notwithstanding the provisions of section 4(1); ...

(3) If at any stage in any proceedings before a judicial authority in Great Britain (not being proceedings to which, by virtue of any of paragraphs (a) to (e) of subsection (2) above or of any order for the time being in force under subsection (4) below, section 4(1) above has no application, or proceedings to which section 8 below applies) the authority is satisfied in the light of any considerations which appears to it to be relevant (including any evidence which has been or may thereafter be put before it), that justice cannot be done in the case except by admitting or requiring evidence relating to a person's spent convictions or to circumstances ancillary thereto, that authority may admit or, as the case may be, require the evidence in question notwithstanding the provisions of subsection (1) of section 4 above, and may determine any issue to which the evidence relates in disregard, so far as necessary, of those provisions.

(4) The Secretary of State may by order exclude the application of section 4(1) above in relation to any proceedings specified in the order (other than proceedings to which section 8 below applies) to such extent and for such purposes as may be so specified.

(5) No order made by a court with respect to any person otherwise than on a conviction shall be included in any list or statement of that person's previous convictions given or made to any court which is considering how to deal with him in respect of any offence.

8 Defamation actions

(1) This section applies to any action for libel or slander begun after the commencement of this Act by a rehabilitated person and founded upon the publication of any matter imputing that the plaintiff has committed or been charged with or prosecuted for or convicted of or sentenced for an offence which was the subject of a spent conviction.

(2) Nothing in section 4(1) above shall affect an action to which this section applies where the publication complained of took place before the conviction in question became spent, and the following provisions of this section shall not apply in any such case.

(3) Subject to subsections (5) and (6) below, nothing in section 4(1) above shall prevent the defendant in an action to which this section applies from relying on any defence of justification or fair comment or of absolute or qualified privilege which is available to him, or restrict the matters he may establish in support of any such defence.

(4) Without prejudice to the generality of subsection (3) above, where in any such action malice is alleged against a defendant who is relying on a

defence of qualified privilege, nothing in section 4(1) above shall restrict the matters he may establish in rebuttal of the allegation.

(5) A defendant in any such action shall not by virtue of subsection (3) above be entitled to rely upon the defence of justification if the publication is proved to have been made with malice.

(6) Subject to subsection (7) below a defendant in any such action shall not, by virtue of subsection (3) above, be entitled to rely on any matter or adduce or require any evidence for the purpose of establishing (whether under section 14 of the Defamation Act 1996 or otherwise) the defence that the matter published constituted a fair and accurate report of judicial proceedings if it is proved that the publication contained a reference to evidence which was ruled to be inadmissible in the proceedings by virtue of section 4(1) above.

(7) Subsection (3) above shall apply without the qualifications imposed by subsection (6) above in relation to –

(a) any report of judicial proceedings contained in any bona fide series of law reports which does not form any part of any other publication and consists solely of reports of proceedings in courts of law; and

(b) any report or account of judicial proceedings published for bona fide educational, scientific or professional purposes, or given in the course of any lecture, class or discussion given or held for any of those purposes.

As amended by the Children Act 1989, s108(5), Schedule 13, para 35; Defamation Act 1996, s14(4), from a day to be appointed.

SEXUAL OFFENCES (AMENDMENT) ACT 1976

(1976 c 82)

1 Meaning of 'rape', etc

(2) It is hereby declared that if at a trial for a rape offence the jury has to consider whether a man believed that a woman or man was consenting to sexual intercourse, the presence or absence of reasonable grounds for such a belief is a matter to which the jury is to have regard, in conjunction with any other relevant matters, in considering whether he so believed.

2 Restrictions on evidence at trials for rape, etc

(1) If at a trial any person is for the time being charged with a rape offence to which he pleads not guilty, then, except with the leave of the judge, no evidence and no question in cross-examination shall be adduced or asked at the trial, by or on behalf of any defendant at the trial, about any sexual experience of a complainant with a person other than that defendant.

(2) The judge shall not give leave in pursuance of the preceding subsection for any evidence or question except on an application made to him in the absence of the jury by or on behalf of a defendant; and on such an application the judge shall give leave if and only if he is satisfied that it would be unfair to that defendant to refuse to allow the evidence to be adduced or the question to be asked.

(3) In subsection (1) of this section 'complainant' means a woman or man upon whom, in a charge for a rape offence to which the trial in question relates, it is alleged that rape was committed, attempted or proposed.

(4) Nothing in this section authorises evidence to be adduced or a question to be asked which cannot be adduced or asked apart from this section.

3 Application of s2 to committal proceedings, courts-martial and summary trials

(1) Where a magistrates' court inquires into a rape offence as examining justices, then, except with the consent of the court, no restricted matter shall be raised; and for this purpose a restricted matter is a matter as regards which evidence could not be adduced and a question could not be asked without leave in pursuance of section 2 of this Act if –

(a) the inquiry were a trial at which a person is charged as mentioned in section 2(1) of this Act, and

(b) each of the accused at the inquiry were charged at the trial with the offence or offences of which he is accused at the inquiry.

(2) On an application for consent in pursuance of the preceding subsection for any matter the court shall –

(a) refuse the consent unless the court is satisfied that leave in respect of the matter would be likely to be given at a relevant trial; and

(b) give the consent if the court is so satisfied.

(3) Where a person charged with a rape offence is tried for that offence ... summarily before a magistrates' court in pursuance of section 24(1) of the Magistrates' Courts Act 1980 (which provides for the summary trial in certain cases of persons under the age of 17 who are charged with indictable offences) the preceding section shall have effect in relation to the trial as if –

(a) the words 'in the absence of the jury' in subsection (2) were omitted ... and

(b) for any reference to the judge there were substituted – ...

(ii) ... a reference to the court.

As amended by the Magistrates' Courts Act 1980, s154(1), Schedule 7, para 148; Criminal Justice and Public Order Act 1994, s168(2), (3), Schedule 10, para 35(1) – (3), Schedule 11; Criminal Procedure and Investigations Act 1996, s47, Schedule 1, Pt II, para 23.

OATHS ACT 1978
(1978 c 19)

PART I

ENGLAND, WALES AND NORTHERN IRELAND

1 Manner of administration of oaths

(1) Any oath may be administered and taken in England, Wales or Northern Ireland in the following form and manner –

The person taking the oath shall hold the New Testament, or, in the case of a Jew, the Old Testament, in his uplifted hand, and shall say or repeat after the officer administering the oath the words 'I swear by Almighty God that ...', followed by the words of the oath prescribed by law.

(2) The officer shall (unless the person about to take the oath voluntarily objects thereto, or is physically incapable of so taking the oath) administer the oath in the form and manner aforesaid without question.

(3) In the case of a person who is neither a Christian nor a Jew, the oath shall be administered in any lawful manner.

(4) In this section 'officer' means any person duly authorised to administer oaths.

PART II

UNITED KINGDOM

3 Swearing with uplifted hand

If any person to whom an oath is administered desires to swear with uplifted hand, in the form and manner in which an oath is usually administered in Scotland, he shall be permitted so to do, and the oath shall be administered to him in such form and manner without further question.

4 Validity of oaths

(1) In any case in which an oath may lawfully be and has been administered to any person, if it has been administered in a form and manner other than that prescribed by law, he is bound by it if it has been administered in such form and with such ceremonies as he may have declared to be binding.

(2) Where an oath has been duly administered and taken, the fact that the person to whom it was administered had, at the time of taking it, no religious belief, shall not for any purpose affect the validity of the oath.

5 Making of solemn affirmations

(1) Any person who objects to being sworn shall be permitted to make his solemn affirmation instead of taking an oath.

(2) Subsection (1) above shall apply in relation to a person to whom it is not reasonably practicable without inconvenience or delay to administer an oath in the manner appropriate to his religious belief as it applies in relation to a person objecting to be sworn.

(3) A person who may be permitted under subsection (2) above to make his solemn affirmation may also be required to do so.

(4) A solemn affirmation shall be of the same force and effect as an oath.

6 Form of affirmation

(1) Subject to subsection (2) below, every affirmation shall be as follows –

> 'I, do solemnly, sincerely and truly declare and affirm,'

and then proceed with the words of the oath prescribed by law, omitting any words of imprecation or calling to witness.

(2) Every affirmation in writing shall commence –

> 'I, of , do solemnly and sincerely affirm,'

and the form in lieu of jurat shall be 'Affirmed at
this day of 19 , before me.'

MAGISTRATES' COURTS ACT 1980
(1980 c 43)

4 General nature of committal proceedings

(1) The functions of examining justices may be discharged by a single justice.

(2) Examining justices shall sit in open court except where any enactment contains an express provision to the contrary and except where it appears to them as respects the whole or any part of committal proceedings that the ends of justice would not be served by their sitting in open court.

(3) Subject to subsection (4) below, evidence tendered before examining justices shall be tendered in the presence of the accused.

(4) Examining justices may allow evidence to be tendered before them in the absence of the accused if –

(a) they consider that by reason of his disorderly conduct before them it is not practicable for the evidence to be tendered in his presence, or

(b) he cannot be present for reasons of health but is represented by a legal representative and has consented to the evidence being tendered in his absence.

5A Evidence which is admissible

(1) Evidence falling within subsection (2) below, and only that evidence, shall be admissible by a magistrates' court inquiring into an offence as examining justices.

(2) Evidence falls within this subsection if it –

(a) is tendered by or on behalf of the prosecutor, and

(b) falls within subsection (3) below.

(3) The following evidence falls within this subsection –

(a) written statements complying with section 5B below;

(b) the documents or other exhibits (if any) referred to in such statements;

(c) depositions complying with section 5C below;

(d) the documents or other exhibits (if any) referred to in such depositions;

(e) statements complying with section 5D below;

(f) documents falling within section 5E below.

(4) In this section 'document' means anything in which information of any description is recorded.

5B Written statements

(1) For the purposes of section 5A above a written statement complies with this section if –

(a) the conditions falling within subsection (2) below are met, and

(b) such of the conditions falling within subsection (3) below as apply are met.

(2) The conditions falling within this subsection are that –

(a) the statement purports to be signed by the person who made it;

(b) the statement contains a declaration by that person to the effect that it is true to the best of his knowledge and belief and that he made the statement knowing that, if it were tendered in evidence, he would be liable to prosecution if he wilfully stated in it anything which he knew to be false or did not believe to be true;

(c) before the statement is tendered in evidence a copy of the statement is given, by or on behalf of the prosecutor, to each of the other parties to the proceedings.

(3) The conditions falling within this subsection are that –

(a) if the statement is made by a person under 18 years old, it gives his age;

(b) if it is made by a person who cannot read it, it is read to him before he signs it and is accompanied by a declaration by the person who so read the statement to the effect that it was so read;

(c) if it refers to any other document as an exhibit, the copy given to any other party to the proceedings under subsection (2)(c) above is accompanied by a copy of that document or by such information as may be necessary to enable the party to whom it is given to inspect that document or a copy of it.

(3A) In the case of a statement which indicates in pursuance of subsection (3)(a) of this section that the person making it has not attained the age of fourteen, subsection (2)(b) of this section shall have effect as if for the words from 'made' onwards there were substituted the words 'understands the importance of telling the truth in it'.

(4) So much of any statement as is admitted in evidence by virtue of this section shall, unless the court commits the accused for trial by virtue of section 6(2) below or the court otherwise directs, be read aloud at the hearing; and where the court so directs an account shall be given orally of so much of any statement as is not read aloud.

(5) Any document or other object referred to as an exhibit and identified in a statement admitted in evidence by virtue of this section shall be treated as if it had been produced as an exhibit and identified in court by the maker of the statement.

(6) In this section 'document' means anything in which information of any description is recorded.

5C Depositions

(1) For the purposes of section 5A above a deposition complies with this section if –

(a) a copy of it is sent to the prosecutor under section 97A(9) below,

(b) the condition falling within subsection (2) below is met, and

(c) the condition falling within subsection (3) below is met, in a case where it applies.

(2) The condition falling within this subsection is that before the magistrates' court begins to inquire into the offence concerned as examining justices a copy of the deposition is given, by or on behalf of the prosecutor, to each of the other parties to the proceedings.

(3) The condition falling within this subsection is that, if the deposition refers to any other document as an exhibit, the copy given to any other party to the proceedings under subsection (2) above is accompanied by a copy of that document or by such information as may be necessary to enable the party to whom it is given to inspect that document or a copy of it.

(4) So much of any deposition as is admitted in evidence by virtue of this section shall, unless the court commits the accused for trial by virtue of section 6(2) below or the court otherwise directs, be read aloud at the hearing; and where the court so directs an account shall be given orally of so much of any deposition as is not read aloud.

(5) Any document or other object referred to as an exhibit and identified in a deposition admitted in evidence by virtue of this section shall be treated as if it had been produced as an exhibit and identified in court by the person whose evidence is taken as the deposition.

(6) In this section 'document' means anything in which information of any description is recorded.

5D Statements

(1) For the purposes of section 5A above a statement complies with this section if the conditions falling within subsections (2) to (4) below are met.

(2) The condition falling within this subsection is that, before the committal proceedings begin, the prosecutor notifies the magistrates' court and each of the other parties to the proceedings that he believes –

(a) that the statement might by virtue of section 23 or 24 of the Criminal Justice Act 1988 (statements in certain documents) be admissible as evidence if the case came to trial, and

(b) that the statement would not be admissible as evidence otherwise than by virtue of section 23 or 24 of that Act if the case came to trial.

(3) The condition falling within this subsection is that –

(a) the prosecutor's belief is based on information available to him at the time he makes the notification,

(b) he has reasonable grounds for his belief, and

(c) he gives the reasons for his belief when he makes the notification.

(4) The condition falling within this subsection is that when the court or a party is notified as mentioned in subsection (2) above a copy of the statement is given, by or on behalf of the prosecutor, to the court or the party concerned.

(5) So much of any statement as is in writing and is admitted in evidence by virtue of this section shall, unless the court commits the accused for trial by virtue of section 6(2) below or the court otherwise directs, be read aloud at the hearing; and where the court so directs an account shall be given orally of so much of any statement as is not read aloud.

5E Other documents

(1) The following documents fall within this section –

(a) any document which by virtue of any enactment is evidence in proceedings before a magistrates' court inquiring into an offence as examining justices;

(b) any document which by virtue of any enactment is admissible, or may be used, or is to be admitted or received, in or as evidence in such proceedings;

(c) any document which by virtue of any enactment may be considered in such proceedings;

(d) any document whose production constitutes proof in such proceedings by virtue of any enactment;

(e) any document by the production of which evidence may be given in such proceedings by virtue of any enactment.

(2) In subsection (1) above –

(a) references to evidence include references to prima facie evidence;

(b) references to any enactment include references to any provision of this Act.

(3) So much of any document as is admitted in evidence by virtue of this section shall, unless the court commits the accused for trial by virtue of section 6(2) below or the court otherwise directs, be read aloud at the hearing; and where the court so directs an account shall be given orally of so much of any document as is not read aloud.

(4) In this section 'document' means anything in which information of any description is recorded.

5F Proof by production of copy

(1) Where a statement, deposition or document is admissible in evidence by virtue of section 5B, 5C, 5D or 5E above it may be proved by the production of –

(a) the statement, deposition or document, or

(b) a copy of it or the material part of it.

(2) Subsection (1)(b) above applies whether or not the statement, deposition or document is still in existence.

(3) It is immaterial for the purposes of this section how many removes there are between a copy and the original.

(4) In this section 'copy', in relation to a statement, deposition or document, means anything onto which information recorded in the statement,

deposition or document has been copied, by whatever means and whether directly or indirectly.

6 Discharge or committal for trial

(1) A magistrates' court inquiring into an offence as examining justices shall on consideration of the evidence –

(a) commit the accused for trial if it is of opinion that there is sufficient evidence to put him on trial by jury for any indictable offence;

(b) discharge him if it is not of that opinion and he is in custody for no other cause than the offence under inquiry;

but the preceding provisions of this subsection have effect subject to the provisions of this and any other Act relating to the summary trial of indictable offences.

(2) If a magistrates' court inquiring into an offence as examining justices is satisfied that all the evidence tendered by or on behalf of the prosecutor falls within section 5A(3) above, it may commit the accused for trial for the offence without consideration of the contents of any statements, depositions or other documents, and without consideration of any exhibits which are not documents, unless –

(a) the accused or one of the accused has no legal representative acting for him in the case, or

(b) a legal representative for the accused or one of the accused, as the case may be, has requested the court to consider a submission that there is insufficient evidence to put that accused on trial by jury for the offence;

and subsection (1) above shall not apply to a committal for trial under this subsection. ...

97 Summons to witness and warrant for his arrest

(1) Where a justice of the peace for any commission area is satisfied that any person is likely to be able to give material evidence, or produce any document or thing likely to be material evidence, at the summary trial of an information or hearing of a complaint by a magistrates' court for that commission area and that that person will not voluntarily attend as a witness or will not voluntarily produce the document or thing, the justice shall issue a summons directed to that person requiring him to attend before the court at the time and place appointed in the summons to give evidence or to produce the document or thing.

(2) If a justice of the peace is satisfied by evidence on oath of the matters mentioned in subsection (1) above, and also that it is probable that a summons under that subsection would not procure the attendance of the person in question, the justice may instead of issuing a summons issue a warrant to arrest that person and bring him before such a court as aforesaid at a time and place specified in the warrant; but a warrant shall not be issued under this subsection where the attendance is required for the hearing of a complaint.

(2A) A summons may also be issued under subsection (1) above if the justice is satisfied that the person in question is outside the British Islands but no warrant shall be issued under subsection (2) above unless the justice is satisfied by evidence on oath that the person in question is in England or Wales.

(2B) A justice may refuse to issue a summons under subsection (1) above in relation to the summary trial of an information if he is not satisfied that an application for the summons was made by a party to the case as soon as reasonably practicable after the accused pleaded not guilty.

(2C) In relation to the summary trial of an information, subsection (2) above shall have effect as if the reference to the matters mentioned in subsection (1) above included a reference to the matter mentioned in subsection (2B) above.

(3) On the failure of any person to attend before a magistrates' court in answer to a summons under this section, if –

(a) the court is satisfied by evidence on oath that he is likely to be able to give material evidence or produce any document or thing likely to be material evidence in the proceedings; and

(b) it is proved on oath, or in such other manner as may be prescribed, that he has been duly served with the summons, and that a reasonable sum has been paid or tendered to him for costs and expenses; and

(c) it appears to the court that there is no just excuse for the failure,

the court may issue a warrant to arrest him and bring him before the court at a time and place specified in the warrant.

(4) If any person attending or brought before a magistrates' court refuses without just excuse to be sworn or give evidence, or to produce any document or thing, the court may commit him to custody until the expiration of such period not exceeding one month as may be specified in the warrant or until he sooner gives evidence or produces the document or thing or impose on him a fine not exceeding £2,500, or both. ...

97A Summons or warrant as to committal proceedings

(1) Subsection (2) below applies where a justice of the peace for any commission area is satisfied that –

(a) any person in England or Wales is likely to be able to make on behalf of the prosecutor a written statement containing material evidence, or produce on behalf of the prosecutor a document or other exhibit likely to be material evidence, for the purposes of proceedings before a magistrates' court inquiring into an offence as examining justices,

(b) the person will not voluntarily make the statement or produce the document or other exhibit, and

(c) the magistrates' court mentioned in paragraph (a) above is a court for the commission area concerned.

(2) In such a case the justice shall issue a summons directed to that person requiring him to attend before a justice at the time and place appointed in the summons to have his evidence taken as a deposition or to produce the document or other exhibit.

(3) If a justice of the peace is satisfied by evidence on oath of the matters mentioned in subsection (1) above, and also that it is probable that a summons under subsection (2) above would not procure the result required by it, the justice may instead of issuing a summons issue a warrant to arrest the person concerned and bring him before a justice at the time and place specified in the warrant.

(4) A summons may also be issued under subsection (2) above if the justice is satisfied that the person concerned is outside the British Islands, but no warrant may be issued under subsection (3) above unless the justice is satisfied by evidence on oath that the person concerned is in England or Wales.

(5) If –

(a) a person fails to attend before a justice in answer to a summons under this section,

(b) the justice is satisfied by evidence on oath that he is likely to be able to make a statement or produce a document or other exhibit as mentioned in subsection (1)(a) above,

(c) it is proved on oath, or in such other manner as may be prescribed, that he has been duly served with the summons and that a reasonable sum has been paid or tendered to him for costs and expenses, and

(d) it appears to the justice that there is no just excuse for the failure, the justice may issue a warrant to arrest him and bring him before a justice at a time and place specified in the warrant.

(6) Where –

(a) a summons is issued under subsection (2) above or a warrant is issued under subsection (3) or (5) above, and

(b) the summons or warrant is issued with a view to securing that a person has his evidence taken as a deposition,

the time appointed in the summons or specified in the warrant shall be such as to enable the evidence to be taken as a deposition before a magistrates' court begins to inquire into the offence concerned as examining justices.

(7) If any person attending or brought before a justice in pursuance of this section refuses without just excuse to have his evidence taken as a deposition, or to produce the document or other exhibit, the justice may do one or both of the following –

(a) commit him to custody until the expiration of such period not exceeding one month as may be specified in the summons or warrant or until he sooner has his evidence taken as a deposition or produces the document or other exhibit;

(b) impose on him a fine not exceeding £2,500. ...

98 Evidence on oath

Subject to the provisions of any enactment or rule of law authorising the reception of unsworn evidence, evidence given before a magistrates' court shall be given on oath.

101 Onus of proving exceptions, etc

Where the defendant to an information or complaint relies for his defence on any exception, exemption, proviso, excuse or qualification, whether or not it accompanies the description of the offence or matter of complaint in the enactment creating the offence or on which the complaint is founded, the burden of proving the exception, exemption, proviso, excuse or qualification shall be on him; and this notwithstanding that the information or complaint contains an allegation negativing the exception, exemption, proviso, excuse or qualification.

103 Evidence of persons under 14 in committal proceedings for assault, sexual offences, etc

(1) In any proceedings before a magistrates' court inquiring as examining justices into an offence to which this section applies, a statement made in writing by or taken in writing from a child shall be admissible in evidence of any matter.

(2) This section applies –

(a) to an offences which involves an assault, or injury or a threat of injury to, a person;

(b) to an offence under section 1 of the Children and Young Persons Act 1933 (cruelty to persons under 16);

(c) to an offence under the Sexual Offences Act 1956, the Indecency with Children Act 1960, the Sexual Offences Act 1967, section 54 of the Criminal Law Act 1977 or the Protection of Children Act 1978; and

(d) to an offence which consists of attempting or conspiring to commit, or of aiding, abetting, counselling, procuring or inciting the commission of, an offence falling within paragraph (a), (b), or (c) above.

104 Proof of previous convictions

Where a person is convicted of a summary offence by a magistrates' court, other than a youth court, and –

(a) it is proved to the satisfaction of the court, on oath or in such other manner as may be prescribed, that not less than seven days previously a notice was served on the accused in the prescribed form and manner specifying any alleged previous conviction of the accused of a summary offence proposed to be brought to the notice of the court in the event of his conviction of the offence charged; and

(b) the accused is not present in person before the court,

the court may take account of any such previous conviction so specified as if the accused had appeared and admitted it.

As amended or substituted by the Children and Young Persons Act 1969, s72(3), Schedule 5, para 55; Contempt of Court Act 1981, s14, Schedule 2, Pt III, para 7; Criminal Justice Act 1988, s33; Courts and Legal Services Act 1990, s125(3), Schedule 18, para 25(1), (3)(a); Criminal Justice (International Co-operation) Act 1990, s31(1), Schedule 4, para 2; Criminal Justice Act 1991, ss17(3)(a), (e), 70, 100, Schedule 4, Pt I, Pt V, para 2, Schedule 11, para 40(1), (2)(n); Criminal Procedure and Investigations Act 1996, ss47, 51(1), (2), 80, Schedule 1, Pt I, paras 1–4, 7, 8, 10, Pt II, para 21, Schedule 5(10); Magistrates' Courts (Wales) (Consequences of Local Government Changes) Order 1996, art 2, Schedule, Pt I, para 2(4), (5).

CONTEMPT OF COURT ACT 1981

(1981 c 49)

10 Sources of information

No court may require a person to disclose, nor is any person guilty of contempt of court for refusing to disclose, the source of information contained in a publication for which he is responsible, unless it be established to the satisfaction of the court that disclosure is necessary in the interests of justice or national security or for the prevention of disorder or crime.

SUPREME COURT ACT 1981

(1981 c 54)

72 Withdrawal of privilege against incrimination of self or spouse in certain proceedings

(1) In any proceedings to which this subsection applies a person shall not be excused, by reason that to do so would tend to expose that person, or his or her spouse, to proceedings for a related offence of for the recovery of a related penalty –

(a) from answering any question put to that person in the first-mentioned proceedings; or

(b) from complying with any order made in those proceedings.

(2) Subsection (1) applies to the following civil proceedings in the High Court, namely –

(a) proceedings for infringement of rights pertaining to any intellectual property or for passing off;

(b) proceedings brought to obtain disclosure of information relating to any infringement of such rights or to any passing off; and

(c) proceedings brought to prevent any apprehended infringement of such rights or any apprehended passing off.

(3) Subject to subsection (4), no statement or admission made by a person –

(a) in answering a question put to him in any proceedings to which subsection (1) applies; or

(b) in complying with any order made in any such proceedings,

shall, in proceedings for any related offence or for the recovery of any related penalty, be admissible in evidence against that person or (unless they married after the making of the statement or admission) against the spouse of that person.

(4) Nothing in subsection (3) shall render any statement or admission made by a person as there mentioned inadmissible in evidence against that person in proceedings for perjury or contempt of court.

(5) In this section –

'intellectual property' means any patent, trade mark, copyright, design right, registered design, technical or commercial information or other intellectual property;

'related offence', in relation to any proceedings to which subsection (1) applies, means –

(a) in the case of proceedings within subsection (2)(a) or (b) –

(i) any offence committed by or in the course of the infringement or passing off to which those proceedings relate; or

(ii) any offence not within sub-paragraph (i) committed in connection with that infringement or passing off, being an offence involving fraud or dishonesty;

(b) in the case of proceedings within subsection (2)(c), any offence revealed by the facts on which the plaintiff relies in those proceedings;

'related penalty', in relation to any proceedings to which subsection (1) applies means –

(a) in the case of proceedings within subsection (2)(a) or (b), any penalty incurred in respect of anything done or omitted in connection with the infringement or passing off to which those proceedings relate;

(b) in the case of proceedings within subsection (2)(c), any penalty incurred in respect of any act or omission revealed by the facts on which the plaintiff relies in those proceedings.

(6) Any reference in this section to civil proceedings in the High Court of any description includes a reference to proceedings on appeal arising out of civil proceedings in the High Court of that description.

As amended by the Copyright, Designs and Patents Act 1988, s303(1), Schedule 7, para 28.

ROAD TRAFFIC REGULATION ACT 1984

(1984 c 27)

89 Speeding offences generally

(1) A person who drives a motor vehicle on a road at a speed exceeding a limit imposed by or under any enactment to which this section applies shall be guilty of an offence.

(2) A person prosecuted for such an offence shall not be liable to be convicted solely on the evidence of one witness to the effect that, in the opinion of the witness, the person prosecuted was driving the vehicle at a speed exceeding a specified limit. ...

(4) If a person who employs other persons to drive motor vehicles on roads publishes or issues any time-table or schedule, or gives any directions, under which any journey, or any stage or part of any journey, is to be completed within some specified time, and it is not practicable in the circumstances of the case for that journey (or that stage or part of it) to be completed in the specified time without the commission of such an offence as is mentioned in subsection (1) above, the publication or issue of the time-table or schedule, or the giving of the directions may be produced as prima facie evidence that the employer procured or (as the case may be) incited the persons employed by him to drive the vehicles to commit such an offence.

COUNTY COURTS ACT 1984
(1984 c 28)

55 Penalty for neglecting or refusing to give evidence

(1) Subject to subsections (2) and (3), any person who –

(a) having been summoned in pursuance of county court rules as a witness in a county court refuses or neglects, without sufficient cause, to appear or to produce any documents required by the summons to be produced; or

(b) having been so summoned or being present in court and being required to give evidence, refuses to be sworn or give evidence,

shall forfeit such fine as the judge may direct.

(2) A judge shall not have power under subsection (1) to direct that a person shall forfeit a fine of an amount exceeding £1,000.

(3) No person summoned in pursuance of county court rules as a witness in a county court shall forfeit a fine under this section unless there has been paid or tendered to him at the time of the service of the summons such sum in respect of his expenses (including, in such cases as may be prescribed, compensation for loss of time) as may be prescribed for the purposes of this section.

(4) The judge may at his discretion direct that the whole or any part of any such fine, after deducting the costs, shall be applicable towards indemnifying the party injured by the refusal or neglect. ...

58 Persons who may take affidavits for use in county courts

(1) An affidavit to be used in a county court may be sworn before –

(a) the judge or registrar of any court; or

(b) any justice of the peace; or

(c) an officer of any court appointed by the judge of that court for the purpose, as well as before a commissioner for oaths or any other person authorised to take affidavits under the Commissioners for Oaths Acts 1889 and 1891.

(2) An affidavit sworn before a judge or registrar or before any such officer may be sworn without the payment of any fee.

As amended by the Administration of Justice Act 1985, s67(1), (2), Schedule 7, para 8, Schedule 8, Pt II; Criminal Justice Act 1991, s17(3)(a), Schedule 4, Pt I.

POLICE AND CRIMINAL EVIDENCE ACT 1984

(1984 c 60)

PART V

QUESTIONING AND TREATMENT OF PERSONS BY POLICE

58 Access to legal advice

(1) A person arrested and held in custody in a police station or other premises shall be entitled, if he so requests, to consult a solicitor privately at any time.

(2) Subject to subsection (3) below, a request under subsection (1) above and at the time at which it was made shall be recorded in the custody record.

(3) Such a request need not be recorded in the custody record of a person who makes it at a time while he is at a court after being charged with an offence.

(4) If a person makes such a request, he must be permitted to consult a solicitor as soon as is practicable except to the extent that delay is permitted by this section.

(5) In any case he must be permitted to consult a solicitor within 36 hours from the relevant time, as defined in section 41(2) above.

(6) Delay in compliance with a request is only permitted –

(a) in the case of a person who is in police detention for a serious arrestable offence; and

(b) if an officer of at least the rank of superintendent authorises it.

(7) An officer may give an authorisation under subsection (6) above orally or in writing but, if he gives it orally, he shall confirm it in writing as soon as is practicable.

(8) Subject to subsection (8A) below an officer may only authorise delay where he has reasonable grounds for believing that the exercise of the right conferred by subsection (1) above at the time when the person detained desires to exercise it –

(a) will lead to interference with or harm to evidence connected with a serious arrestable offence or interference with or physical injury to other persons; or

(b) will lead to the alerting of other persons suspected of having committed such an offence but not yet arrested for it; or

(c) will hinder the recovery of any property obtained as a result of such an offence.

(8A) An officer may also authorise delay where the serious arrestable offence is a drug trafficking offence or an offence to which Part VI of the Criminal Justice Act 1988 applies and the officer has reasonable grounds for believing –

(a) where the offence is a drug trafficking offence, that the detained person has benefited from drug trafficking and that the recovery of the value of that person's proceeds of drug trafficking will be hindered by the exercise of the right conferred by subsection (1) above; and

(b) where the offence is one to which Part VI of the Criminal Justice Act 1988 applies, that the detained person has benefited from the offence and that the recovery of the value of the property obtained by that person from or in connection with the offence or of the pecuniary advantage derived by him from or in connection with it will be hindered by the exercise of the right conferred by subsection (1) above.

(9) If delay is authorised –

(a) the detained person shall be told the reason for it; and

(b) the reason shall be noted on his custody record.

(10) The duties imposed by subsection (9) above shall be performed as soon as is practicable.

(11) There may be no further delay in permitting the exercise of the right conferred by subsection (1) above once the reason for authorising delay ceases to subsist.

(12) The reference in subsection (1) above to a person arrested includes a reference to a person who has been detained under the terrorism provisions.

(13) In the application of this section to a person who has been arrested or detained under the terrorism provisions –

(a) subsection (5) above shall have effect as if for the words from 'within' onwards there were substituted the words 'before the end of the period beyond which he may no longer be detained without the authority of the Secretary of State';

(b) subsection (6)(a) above shall have effect as if for the words 'for a serious arrestable offence' there were substituted the words 'under the terrorism provisions'; and

(c) subsection (8) above shall have effect as if at the end there were added; or

(d) will lead to interference with the gathering of information about the commission, preparation or instigation of acts of terrorism; or

(e) by alerting any person, will make it more difficult –

(i) to prevent an act of terrorism; or

(ii) to secure the apprehension, prosecution or conviction of any person in connection with the commission, preparation or instigation of an act of terrorism.

(14) If an officer of appropriate rank has reasonable grounds for believing that, unless he gives a direction under subsection (15) below, the exercise by a person arrested or detained under the terrorism provisions of the right conferred by subsection (1) above will have any of the consequences specified in subsection (8) above (as it has effect by virtue of subsection (13) above), he may give a direction under that subsection.

(15) A direction under this subsection is a direction that a person desiring to exercise the right conferred by subsection (1) above may only consult a solicitor in the sight and hearing of a qualified officer of the uniformed branch of the force of which the officer giving the direction is a member.

(16) An officer is qualified for the purpose of subsection (15) above if –

(a) he is of at least the rank of inspector; and

(b) in the opinion of the officer giving the direction he has no connection with the case.

(17) An officer is of appropriate rank to give a direction under subsection (15) above if he is of at least the rank of Commander or Assistant Chief Constable.

(18) A direction under subsection (15) above shall cease to have effect once the reason for giving it ceases to subsist.

PART VII

DOCUMENTARY EVIDENCE IN CRIMINAL PROCEEDINGS

69 Evidence from computer records

(1) In any proceedings, a statement in a document produced by a computer shall not be admissible as evidence of any fact stated therein unless it is shown –

(a) that there are no reasonable grounds for believing that the statement is inaccurate because of improper use of the computer;

(b) that at all material times the computer was operating properly, or if not, that any respect in which it was not operating properly or was out of operation was not such as to affect the production of the document or the accuracy of its contents; and

(c) that any relevant conditions specified in rules of court under subsection (2) below are satisfied.

(2) Provision may be made by rules of court requiring that in any proceedings where it is desired to give a statement in evidence by virtue of this section such information concerning the statement as may be required by the rules shall be provided in such form and at such time as may be so required.

70 Provisions supplementary to sections 68 and 69

(2) Part II of that Schedule [Schedule 3] shall have effect for the purpose of supplementing section 69 above.

(3) Part III of that Schedule shall have effect for the purpose of supplementing both sections.

71 Microfilm copies

In any proceedings the contents of a document may (whether or not the document is still in existence) be proved by the production of an enlargement of a microfilm copy of that document or of the material part of it, authenticated in such manner as the court may approve.

Where the proceedings concerned are proceedings before a magistrates' court inquiring into an offence as examining justices this section shall have effect with the omission of the words 'authenticated in such manner as the court may approve'.

72 Part VII – supplementary

(1) In this Part of this Act –

'copy', in relation to a document, means anything onto which information recorded in the document has been copied, by whatever means and whether directly or indirectly, and 'statement' means any representation of fact, however made;

'proceedings' means criminal proceedings, including –

(a) proceedings in the United Kingdom or elsewhere before a court-martial constituted under the Army Act 1955, the Air Force Act 1955 or the Naval Discipline Act 1957;

(b) proceedings in the United Kingdom or elsewhere before the Courts-Martial Appeal Court –

(i) on an appeal from a court-martial so constituted; or

(ii) on a reference under section 34 of the Courts-Martial (Appeals) Act 1968; and

(c) proceedings before a Standing Civilian Court.

(2) Nothing in this Part of this Act shall prejudice any power of a court to exclude evidence (whether by preventing questions from being put or otherwise) at its discretion.

PART VIII

EVIDENCE IN CRIMINAL PROCEEDINGS – GENERAL

73 Proof of convictions and acquittals

(1) Where in any proceedings the fact that a person has in the United Kingdom been convicted or acquitted of an offence otherwise than by a Service court is admissible in evidence, it may be proved by producing a certificate of conviction or, as the case may be, of acquittal relating to that offence, and proving that the person named in the certificate as having been convicted or acquitted of the offence is the person whose conviction or acquittal of the offence is to be proved.

(2) For the purposes of this section a certificate of conviction or of acquittal –

(a) shall, as regards a conviction or acquittal on indictment, consist of a certificate, signed by the clerk of the court where the conviction or acquittal took place, giving the substance and effect (omitting the formal parts) of the indictment and of the conviction or acquittal; and

(b) shall, as regards a conviction or acquittal on a summary trial, consist of a copy of the conviction or of the dismissal of the information, signed by the clerk of the court where the conviction or acquittal took place or by the clerk of the court, if any, to which a memorandum of the conviction or acquittal was sent;

and a document purporting to be a duly signed certificate of conviction or acquittal under this section shall be taken to be such a certificate unless the contrary is proved.

(3) References in this section to the clerk of a court include references to his deputy and to any other person having the custody of the court record.

(4) The method of proving a conviction or acquittal authorised by this section shall be in addition to and not to the exclusion of any other authorised manner of proving a conviction or acquittal.

74 Conviction as evidence of commission of offence

(1) In any proceedings the fact that a person other than the accused has been convicted of an offence by or before any court in the United Kingdom or by a Service court outside the United Kingdom shall be admissible in evidence for the purpose of proving, where to do so is relevant to any issue in those proceedings, that that person committed that offence, whether or not any other evidence of his having committed that offence is given.

(2) In any proceedings in which by virtue of this section a person other than the accused is proved to have been convicted of an offence by or before any court in the United Kingdom or by a Service court outside the United Kingdom, he shall be taken to have committed that offence unless the contrary is proved.

(3) In any proceedings where evidence is admissible of the fact that the accused has committed an offence, in so far as that evidence is relevant to any matter in issue in the proceedings for a reason other than a tendency to show in the accused a disposition to commit the kind of offence with which he is charged, if the accused is proved to have been convicted of the offence –

(a) by or before any court in the United Kingdom; or

(b) by a Service court outside the United Kingdom,

he shall be taken to have committed that offence unless the contrary is proved.

(4) Nothing in this section shall prejudice –

(a) the admissibility in evidence of any conviction which would be admissible apart from this section; or

(b) the operation of any enactment whereby a conviction or a finding of fact in any proceedings is for the purposes of any other proceedings made conclusive evidence of any fact.

75 Provisions supplementary to section 74

(1) Where evidence that a person has been convicted of an offence is admissible by virtue of section 74 above, then without prejudice to the reception of any other admissible evidence for the purpose of identifying the facts on which the conviction was based –

(a) the contents of any document which is admissible as evidence of the conviction; and

(b) the contents of the information, complaint, indictment or charge-sheet on which the person in question was convicted,

shall be admissible in evidence for that purpose.

(2) Where in any proceedings the contents of any document are admissible in evidence by virtue of subsection (1) above, a copy of that document, or of the material part of it, purporting to be certified or otherwise authenticated by or on behalf of the court or authority having custody of that document shall be admissible in evidence and shall be taken to be a true copy of that document or part unless the contrary is shown.

(3) Nothing in any of the following –

(a) section 13 of the Powers of Criminal Courts Act 1973 (under which a conviction leading to probation or discharge is to be disregarded except as mentioned in that section); ...

shall affect the operation of section 74 above ...

(4) Nothing in section 74 above shall be construed as rendering admissible in any proceedings evidence of any conviction other than a subsisting one.

76 Confessions

(1) In any proceedings a confession made by an accused person may be given in evidence against him in so far as it is relevant to any matter in issue in the proceedings and is not excluded by the court in pursuance of this section.

(2) If, in any proceedings where the prosecution proposes to give in evidence

a confession made by an accused person, it is represented to the court that the confession was or may have been obtained –

(a) by oppression of the person who made it; or

(b) in consequence of anything said or done which was likely, in the circumstances existing at the time, to render unreliable any confession which might be made by him in consequence thereof,

the court shall not allow the confession to be given in evidence against him except in so far as the prosecution proves to the court beyond reasonable doubt that the confession (notwithstanding that it may be true) was not obtained as aforesaid.

(3) In any proceedings where the prosecution proposes to give in evidence a confession made by an accused person, the court may of its own motion require the prosecution, as a condition of allowing it to do so, to prove that the confession was not obtained as mentioned in subsection (2) above.

(4) The fact that a confession is wholly or partly excluded in pursuance of this section shall not affect the admissibility in evidence –

(a) of any facts discovered as a result of the confession; or

(b) where the confession is relevant as showing that the accused speaks, writes or expresses himself in a particular way, of so much of the confession as is necessary to show that he does so.

(5) Evidence that a fact to which this subsection applies was discovered as a result of a statement made by an accused person shall not be admissible unless evidence of how it was discovered is given by him or on his behalf.

(6) Subsection (5) above applies –

(a) to any fact discovered as a result of a confession which is wholly excluded in pursuance of this section; and

(b) to any fact discovered as a result of a confession which is partly so excluded, if the fact is discovered as a result of the excluded part of the confession.

(7) Nothing in Part VII of this Act shall prejudice the admissibility of a confession made by an accused person.

(8) In this section 'oppression' includes torture, inhuman or degrading treatment, and the use or threat of violence (whether or not amounting to torture).

(9) Where the proceedings mentioned in subsection (1) above are proceedings before a magistrates' court inquiring into an offence as examining justices this section shall have effect with the omission of –

(a) in subsection (1) the words 'and is not excluded by the court in pursuance of this section', and

(b) subsections (2) to (6) and (8).

77 Confessions by mentally handicapped persons

(1) Without prejudice to the general duty of the court at a trial on indictment to direct the jury on any matter on which it appears to the court appropriate to do so, where at such a trial –

(a) the case against the accused depends wholly or substantially on a confession by him; and

(b) the court is satisfied –

(i) that he is mentally handicapped; and

(ii) that the confession was not made in the presence of an independent person,

the court shall warn the jury that there is special need for caution before convicting the accused in reliance on the confession, and shall explain that the need arises because of the circumstances mentioned in paragraphs (a) and (b) above.

(2) In any case where at the summary trial of a person for an offence it appears to the court that a warning under subsection (1) above would be required if the trial were on indictment, the court shall treat the case as one in which there is a special need for caution before convicting the accused on his confession.

(3) In this section –

'independent person' does not include a police officer or a person employed for, or engaged on, police purposes;

'mentally handicapped', in relation to a person, means that he is in a state of arrested or incomplete development of mind which includes significant impairment of intelligence and social functioning; and

'police purposes' has the meaning assigned to it by section 101(2) of the Police Act 1996.

78 Exclusion of unfair evidence

(1) In any proceedings the court may refuse to allow evidence on which the prosecution proposes to rely to be given if it appears to the court that, having regard to all the circumstances, including the circumstances in

which the evidence was obtained, the admission of the evidence would have such an adverse effect on the fairness of the proceedings that the court ought not to admit it.

(2) Nothing in this section shall prejudice any rule of law requiring a court to exclude evidence.

(3) This section shall not apply in the case of proceedings before a magistrates' court inquiring into an offence as examining justices.

79 Time for taking accused's evidence

If at the trial of any person for an offence –

(a) the defence intends to call two or more witnesses to the facts of the case; and

(b) those witnesses include the accused,

the accused shall be called before the other witness or witnesses unless the court in its discretion otherwise directs.

80 Competence and compellability of accused's spouse

(1) In any proceedings the wife or husband of the accused shall be competent to give evidence –

(a) subject to subsection (4) below, for the prosecution; and

(b) on behalf of the accused or any person jointly charged with the accused.

(2) In any proceedings the wife or husband of the accused shall, subject to subsection (4) below, be compellable to give evidence on behalf of the accused.

(3) In any proceedings the wife or husband of the accused shall, subject to subsection (4) below, be compellable to give evidence for the prosecution or on behalf of any person jointly charged with the accused if and only if –

(a) the offence charged involves an assault on, or injury or a threat of injury to, the wife or husband of the accused or a person who was at the material time under the age of sixteen; or

(b) the offence charged is a sexual offence alleged to have been committed in respect of a person who was at the material time under that age; or

(c) the offence charged consists of attempting or conspiring to commit, or of aiding, abetting, counselling, procuring or inciting the commission of, an offence falling within paragraph (a) or (b) above.

(4) Where a husband and wife are jointly charged with an offence neither spouse shall at the trial be competent or compellable by virtue of subsections (1)(a), (2) or (3) above to give evidence in respect of that offence unless that spouse is not, or is no longer, liable to be convicted of that offence at the trial as a result of pleading guilty or for any other reason.

(5) In any proceedings a person who has been but is no longer married to the accused shall be competent and compellable to give evidence as if that person and the accused had never been married.

(6) Where in any proceedings the age of any person at any time is material for the purposes of subsection (3) above, his age at the material time shall for the purposes of that provision be deemed to be or to have been that which appears to the court to be or to have been his age at that time.

(7) In subsection (3)(b) above 'sexual offence' means an offence under the Sexual Offences Act 1956, the Indecency with Children Act 1960, the Sexual Offences Act 1967, section 54 of the Criminal Law Act 1977 or the Protection of Children Act 1978.

(8) The failure of the wife or husband of the accused to give evidence shall not be made the subject of any comment by the prosecution.

81 Advance notice of expert evidence in Crown Court

(1) Crown Court Rules may make provision for –

(a) requiring any party to proceedings before the court to disclose to the other party or parties any expert evidence which he proposes to adduce in the proceedings; and

(b) prohibiting a party who fails to comply in respect of any evidence with any requirement imposed by virtue of paragraph (a) above from adducing that evidence without the leave of the court.

(2) Crown Court Rules made by virtue of this section may specify the kinds of expert evidence to which they apply and may exempt facts or matters of any description specified in the rules.

82 Part VIII – interpretation

(1) In this Part of this Act –

'confession' includes any statement wholly or partly adverse to the person who made it, whether made to a person in authority or not and whether made in words or otherwise;

'court-martial' means a court-martial constituted under the Army Act 1955, the Air Force Act 1955 or the Naval Discipline Act 1957 or a disciplinary court constituted under section 52G of the said Act of 1957;

'proceedings' means criminal proceedings, including –

(a) proceedings in the United Kingdom or elsewhere before a court-martial constituted under the Army Act 1955, the Air Force Act 1955 or the Naval Discipline Act 1957;

(b) proceedings in the United Kingdom or elsewhere before the Courts-Martial Appeal Court –

(i) on an appeal from a court-martial so constituted; or

(ii) on a reference under section 34 of the Courts-Martial (Appeals) Act 1968; and

(c) proceedings before a Standing Civilian Court; and

'Service court' means a court-martial or a Standing Civilian Court.

(2) In this Part of this Act references to conviction before a Service court are references to a finding of guilty which is, or falls to be treated as, the finding of the court;

and 'convicted' shall be construed accordingly.

(3) Nothing in this Part of this Act shall prejudice any power of a court to exclude evidence (whether by preventing questions from being put or otherwise) at its discretion.

PART XI

MISCELLANEOUS AND SUPPLEMENTARY

113 Application of Act to Armed Forces

(12) Parts VII and VIII of this Act have effect for the purposes of proceedings –

(a) before a court-martial constituted under the Army Act 1955 or the Air Force Act 1955;

(b) before the Courts-Martial Appeal Court; and

(c) before a Standing Civilian Court,

subject to any modifications which the Secretary of State may by order specify.

118 General interpretation

(1) In this Act – ...

'document' means anything in which information of any description is recorded; ...

SCHEDULE 3

PART II

PROVISIONS SUPPLEMENTARY TO SECTION 69

8. In any proceedings where it is desired to give a statement in evidence in accordance with section 69 above, a certificate –

(a) identifying the document containing the statement and describing the manner in which it was produced;

(b) giving such particulars of any device involved in the production of that document as may be appropriate for the purpose of showing that the document was produced by a computer;

(c) dealing with any of the matters mentioned in subsection (1) of section 69 above; and

(d) purporting to be signed by a person occupying a responsible position in relation to the operation of the computer,

shall be evidence of anything stated in it; and for the purposes of this paragraph it shall be sufficient for a matter to be stated to the best of the knowledge and belief of the person stating it.

9. Notwithstanding paragraph 8 above, a court may require oral evidence to be given of anything of which evidence could be given by a certificate under that paragraph; but the preceding provisions of this paragraph shall not apply where the court is a magistrates' court inquiring into an offence as examining justices.

10. Any person who in a certificate tendered under paragraph 8 above in a magistrates' court, the Crown Court or the Court of Appeal makes a statement which he knows to be false or does not believe to be true shall be guilty of an offence and liable –

(a) on conviction on indictment to imprisonment for a term not exceeding two years or to a fine or to both;

(b) on summary conviction to imprisonment for a term not exceeding six months or to a fine not exceeding the statutory maximum or to both.

11. In estimating the weight, if any, to be attached to a statement regard shall be had to all the circumstances from which any inference can reasonably be drawn as to the accuracy or otherwise of the statement and, in particular –

(a) to the question whether or not the information which the information contained in the statement reproduces or is derived from was supplied to the relevant computer, or recorded for the purpose of being supplied to it, contemporaneously with the occurrence or existence of the facts dealt with in that information; and

(b) to the question whether or not any person concerned with the supply of information to that computer, or with the operation of that computer or any equipment by means of which the document containing the statement was produced by it, had any incentive to conceal or misrepresent the facts.

12. For the purposes of paragraph 11 above information shall be taken to be supplied to a computer whether it is supplied directly or (with or without human intervention) by means of any appropriate equipment.

PART III

PROVISIONS SUPPLEMENTARY TO SECTIONS 68 AND 69

14. For the purpose of deciding whether or not a statement is so admissible the court may draw any reasonable inference –

(a) from the circumstances in which the statement was made or otherwise came into being; or

(b) from any other circumstances, including the form and contents of the document in which the statement is contained.

15. Provision may be made by rules of court for supplementing the provisions of section 68 or 69 above or this Schedule.

NB. Section 68 was repealed by the Criminal Justice Act 1988, s170(2), Schedule 16. See now s24 of the 1988 Act, below.

As amended by the Drug Trafficking Offences Act 1986, s32(2); Criminal Justice Act 1988, s99(1), (3); Statute Law (Repeals) Act 1993, s1(1), Schedule 1, Pt XIV; Civil Evidence Act 1995, s15(1), Schedule 1, para 9(1)–(3); Criminal Procedure and Investigations Act 1996, s47, Schedule 1, Pt II, paras 24–27; Armed Forces Act 1996, ss5, 35(2), Schedule 1, Pt IV, paras 104, 106, 107, Schedule 6, para 14, Schedule 7, Pt I; Police Act 1996, s103(1), Schedule 7, Pt II, para 38.

INTERCEPTION OF COMMUNICATIONS ACT 1985

(1985 c 56)

2 Warrants for interception

(1) Subject to the provisions of this section and section 3 below, the Secretary of State may issue a warrant requiring the person to whom it is addressed to intercept, in the course of their transmission by post or by means of a public telecommunication system, such communications as are described in the warrant; and such a warrant may also require the person to whom it is addressed to disclose the intercepted material to such persons and in such manner as are described in the warrant.

(2) The Secretary of State shall not issue a warrant under this section unless he considers that the warrant is necessary –

(a) in the interests of national security;

(b) for the purpose of preventing or detecting serious crime; or

(c) for the purpose of safeguarding the economic well-being of the United Kingdom.

(3) The matters to be taken into account in considering whether a warrant is necessary as mentioned in subsection (2) above shall include whether the information which it is considered necessary to acquire could reasonably be acquired by other means.

(4) A warrant shall not be considered necessary as mentioned in subsection (2)(c) above unless the information which it is considered necessary to acquire is information relating to the acts or intentions of persons outside the British Islands. …

3 Scope of warrants

(1) Subject to subsection (2) below, the interception required by a warrant shall be the interception of –

(a) such communications as are sent to or from one or more addresses specified in the warrant, being an address or addresses likely to be used for the transmission of communications to or from –

(i) one particular person specified or described in the warrant; or

(ii) one particular set of premises so specified or described; and

(b) such other communications (if any) as it is necessary to intercept in order to intercept communications falling within paragraph (a) above.

(2) Subsection (1) above shall not apply to a warrant if –

(a) the interception required by the warrant is the interception, in the course of their transmission by means of a public telecommunication system, of –

(i) such external communications as are described in the warrant; and

(ii) such other communications (if any) as it is necessary to intercept in order to intercept such external communications as are so described; and

(b) at the time when the warrant is issued, the Secretary of State issues a certificate certifying the descriptions of intercepted material the examination of which he considers necessary as mentioned in section 2(2) above.

(3) A certificate such as is mentioned in subsection (2) above shall not specify an address in the British Islands for the purpose of including communications sent to or from that address in the certified material unless –

(a) the Secretary of State considers that the examination of communications sent to or from that address is necessary for the purpose of preventing or detecting acts of terrorism; and

(b) communications sent to or from that address are included in the certified material only in so far as they are sent within such a period, not exceeding three months, as is specified in the certificate. ...

BANKING ACT 1987

(1987 c 22)

95 Restriction of Rehabilitation of Offenders Act 1974

(1) The Rehabilitation of Offenders Act 1974 shall have effect subject to the provisions of this section in cases where the spent conviction is for –

(a) an offence involving fraud or other dishonesty; or

(b) an offence under legislation (whether or not of the United Kingdom) relating to companies (including insider dealing), building societies, industrial and provident societies, credit unions, friendly societies, insurance, banking or other financial services, insolvency, consumer credit or consumer protection.

(2) Nothing in section 4(1) (restriction on evidence as to spent convictions in proceedings) shall prevent the determination in any proceeding arising out of any such decision of the Bank as is mentioned in section 27(1) or (3) above (including proceedings on appeal to any court) of any issue, or prevent the admission or requirement in any such proceedings of any evidence, relating to a person's previous convictions for any such offence as is mentioned in subsection (1) above or the circumstances ancillary thereto.

(3) A conviction for such an offence as is mentioned in subsection (1) above shall not be regarded as spent for the purposes of section 4(2) (questions relating to an individual's previous convictions) if –

(a) the question is put by or on behalf of the Bank and the individual is a person who is or is seeking to become a director, controller or manager of an authorised institution, a former authorised institution or an institution which has made an application for authorisation which has not been disposed of; or

(b) the question is put by or on behalf of any such institution and the individual is or is seeking to become a director, controller or manager of that institution,

and the person questioned is informed that by virtue of this section convictions for any such offence are to be disclosed.

(4) Section 4(3)(b) (spent conviction not to be ground for excluding person from office, occupation, etc) shall not –

(a) prevent the Bank from refusing to grant or revoking an authorisation on the ground that an individual is not a fit and proper person to be a director, controller or manager of the institution in question or from imposing a restriction or giving a direction requiring the removal of an individual as director, controller or manager of an institution; or

(b) prevent an authorised institution, a former authorised institution or an institution which has made an application for authorisation which has not yet been disposed of from dismissing or excluding any individual from being a director, controller or manager of the institution,

by reason, or partly by reason, of a spent conviction of that individual for such an offence as is mentioned in subsection (1) above or any circumstances ancillary to such a conviction or of a failure (whether or not by that individual) to disclose such a conviction or any such circumstances.

(5) For the purposes of subsections (3) and (4) above an application by an institution is not disposed of until the decision of the Bank on the application is communicated to the institution.

106 Interpretation

(1) In this Act –

'the Bank' means the Bank of England.

CRIMINAL JUSTICE ACT 1987

(1987 c 38)

7 Powers to order preparatory hearing

(1) Where it appears to a judge of the Crown Court that the evidence on an indictment reveals a case of fraud of such seriousness or complexity that substantial benefits are likely to accrue from a hearing (in this Act referred to as a 'preparatory hearing') before the jury are sworn, for the purpose of –

(a) identifying issues which are likely to be material to the verdict of the jury;

(b) assisting their comprehension of any such issues;

(c) expediting the proceedings before the jury; or

(d) assisting the judge's management of the trial,

he may order that such a hearing shall be held.

(2) A judge may make an order under subsection (1) above on the application either of the prosecution or of the person indicted or, if the indictment charges a number of persons, any of them, or of his own motion.

9 The preparatory hearing

(1) At the preparatory hearing the judge may exercise any of the powers specified in this section.

(2) The judge may adjourn a preparatory hearing from time to time.

(3) He may determine –

(b) any question as to the admissibility of evidence; and

(c) any other question of law relating to the case.

(4) He may order the prosecution –

(a) to supply the court and the defendant or, if there is more than one, each of them with a statement (a 'case statement') of the following –

(i) the principal facts of the prosecution case;

(ii) the witnesses who will speak to those facts;

(iii) any exhibits relevant to those facts;

(iv) any proposition of law on which the prosecution proposes to rely; and

(v) the consequences in relation to any of the counts in the indictment that appear to the prosecution to flow from the matters stated in pursuance of sub-paragraphs (i) to (iv) above;

(b) to prepare their evidence and other explanatory material in such a form as appears to him to be likely to aid comprehension by the jury and to supply it in that form to the court and to the defendant or, if there is more than one, to each of them;

(c) to give the court and the defendant or, if there is more than one, each of them notice of documents the truth of the contents of which ought in the prosecution's view to be admitted and of any other matters which in their view ought to be agreed;

(d) to make any amendments of any case statement supplied in pursuance of an order under paragraph (a) above that appear to the court to be appropriate, having regard to objections made by the defendant or, if there is more than one, by any of them.

(5) Where –

(a) a judge has ordered the prosecution to supply a case statement; and

(b) the prosecution have complied with the order,

he may order the defendant or, if there is more than one, each of them –

(i) to give the court and the prosecution a statement in writing setting out in general terms the nature of his defence and indicating the principal matters on which he takes issue with the prosecution;

(ii) to give the court and the prosecution notice of any objections that he has to the case statement;

(iii) to inform the court and the prosecution of any point of law (including a point as to the admissibility of evidence) which he wishes to take, and any authority on which he intends to rely for that purpose;

(iv) to give the court and the prosecution a notice stating the extent to which he agrees with the prosecution as to documents and other matters to which a notice under subsection (4)(c) above relates and the reason for any disagreements.

(6) Crown Court Rules may provide that except to the extent that disclosure is required –

(a) by section 5(7) of the Criminal Procedure and Investigations Act 1996 (alibi); or

(b) by rules under section 81 of the Police and Criminal Evidence Act 1984 (expert evidence),

a summary required by virtue of subsection (5) above need not disclose who will give evidence ...

(8) If it appears to a judge that reasons given in pursuance of subsection (5)(iv) above are inadequate, he shall so inform the person giving them, and may require him to give further or better reasons.

(9) An order under this section may specify the time within which any specified requirement contained in it is to be compiled with, but Crown Court Rules may make provisions as to the minimum or maximum time that may be specified for compliance.

(10) An order or ruling made under this section shall have effect during the trial, unless it appears to the judge, on application made to him during the trial, that the interests of justice require him to vary or discharge it ...

9A Orders before preparatory hearing

(1) Section (2) below applies where –

(a) a judge orders a preparatory hearing, and

(b) he decides that any order which could be made under section 9(4) or (5) above at the hearing should be made before the hearing.

(2) In such a case –

(a) he may make any such order before the hearing (or at the hearing), and

(b) subsections (4) to (10) of section 9 above shall apply accordingly.

10 Later stages of trial

(1) Any party may depart from the case he disclosed in pursuance of a requirement imposed under section 9 above.

(2) Where –

(a) a party departs from the case he disclosed in pursuance of a requirement imposed under section 9 above, or

(b) a party fails to comply with such a requirement,

the judge or, with the leave of the judge, any other party may make such comment as appears to the judge or the other party (as the case may be) to be appropriate and the jury may draw such inference as appears proper.

(3) In deciding whether to give leave the judge shall have regard –

(a) to the extent of the departure or failure, and

(b) to whether there is any justification for it.

(4) Except as provided by this section no part –

(a) of a statement given under section 9(5) above, or

(b) of any other information relating to the case for the accused or, if there is more than one, the case for any of them, which was given in pursuance of a requirement imposed under section 9 above,

may be disclosed at a stage in the trial after the jury have been sworn without the consent of the accused concerned.

As amended by the Criminal Justice Act 1988, s170(2), Schedule 16; Criminal Justice and Public Order Act 1994, s168(1), Schedule 9, para 30; Criminal Procedure and Investigations Act 1996, ss72, 74(4), (5), 80, Schedule 3, paras 1, 3–5, Schedule 5(12).

CRIMINAL JUSTICE ACT 1988
(1988 c 33)

PART II

DOCUMENTARY EVIDENCE IN CRIMINAL PROCEEDINGS

23 First-hand hearsay

(1) Subject –

(a) to subsection (4) below;

(b) to paragraph 1A of Schedule 2 to the Criminal Appeal Act 1968 (evidence given orally at original trial to be given orally at retrial); and

(c) to section 69 of the Police and Criminal Evidence Act 1984 (evidence from computer records),

a statement made by a person in a document shall be admissible in criminal proceedings as evidence of any fact of which direct oral evidence by him would be admissible if –

(i) the requirements of one of the paragraphs of subsection (2) below are satisfied; or

(ii) the requirements of subsection (3) below are satisfied.

(2) The requirements mentioned in subsection (1)(i) above are –

(a) that the person who made the statement is dead or by reason of his bodily or mental condition unfit to attend as a witness;

(b) that –

(i) the person who made the statement is outside the United Kingdom; and

(ii) it is not reasonably practicable to secure his attendance; or

(c) that all reasonable steps have been taken to find the person who made the statement, but that he cannot be found.

(3) The requirements mentioned in subsection (1)(ii) above are –

(a) that the statement was made to a police officer or some other person charged with the duty of investigating offences or charging offenders; and

(b) that the person who made it does not give oral evidence through fear or because he is kept out of the way.

(4) Subsection (1) above does not render admissible a confession made by an accused person that would not be admissible under section 76 of the Police and Criminal Evidence Act 1984.

(5) This section shall not apply to proceedings before a magistrates' court inquiring into an offence as examining justices.

24 Business, etc documents

(1) Subject –

(a) to subsections (3) and (4) below;

(b) to paragraph 1A of Schedule 2 to the Criminal Appeal Act 1968; and

(c) to section 69 of the Police and Criminal Evidence Act 1984,

a statement in a document shall be admissible in criminal proceedings as evidence of any fact of which direct oral evidence would be admissible, if the following conditions are satisfied –

(i) the document was created or received by a person in the course of a trade, business, profession or other occupation, or as the holder of a paid or unpaid office; and

(ii) the information contained in the document was supplied by a person (whether or not the maker of the statement) who had, or may reasonably be supposed to have had, personal knowledge of the matters dealt with.

(2) Subsection (1) above applies whether the information contained in the document was supplied directly or indirectly but, if it was supplied indirectly, only if each person through whom it was supplied received it –

(a) in the course of a trade, business, profession or other occupation; or

(b) as the holder of a paid or unpaid office.

(3) Subsection (1) above does not render admissible a confession made by an accused person that would not be admissible under section 76 of the Police and Criminal Evidence Act 1984.

(4) A statement prepared otherwise than in accordance with section 3 of the Criminal Justice (International Co-operation) Act 1990 or an order

under paragraph 6 of Schedule 13 to this Act or under section 30 or 31 below for the purposes –

(a) of pending or contemplated criminal proceedings; or

(b) of a criminal investigation,

shall not be admissible by virtue of subsection (1) above unless –

(i) the requirements of one of the paragraphs of subsection (2) of section 23 above are satisfied; or

(ii) the requirements of subsection (3) of that section are satisfied; or

(iii) the person who made the statement cannot reasonably be expected (having regard to the time which has elapsed since he made the statement and to all the circumstances) to have any recollection of the matters dealt with in the statement.

(5) This section shall not apply to proceedings before a magistrates' court inquiring into an offence as examining justices.

25 Principles to be followed by court

(1) If, having regard to all the circumstances –

(a) the Crown Court –

(i) on a trial on indictment;

(ii) on an appeal from a magistrates' court;

(iii) on the hearing of an application under section 6 of the Criminal Justice Act 1987 (applications for dismissal of charges of fraud transferred from magistrates' court to Crown Court); or

(iv) on the hearing of an application under paragraph 5 of Schedule 6 to the Criminal Justice Act 1991 (applications for dismissal of charges in certain cases involving children transferred from magistrates' court to Crown Court); or

(b) the Criminal Division of the Court of Appeal; or

(c) a magistrates' court on a trial of an information,

is of the opinion that in the interests of justice a statement which is admissible by virtue of sections 23 or 24 above nevertheless ought not to be admitted, it may direct that the statement shall not be admitted.

(2) Without prejudice to the generality of subsection (1) above, it shall be the duty of the court to have regard –

(a) to the nature and source of the document containing the statement and to whether or not, having regard to its nature and source and to any other circumstances that appear to the court to be relevant, it is likely that the document is authentic;

(b) to the extent to which the statement appears to supply evidence which would otherwise not be readily available;

(c) to the relevance of the evidence that it appears to supply to any issue which is likely to have to be determined in the proceedings; and

(d) to any risk, having regard in particular to whether it is likely to be possible to controvert the statement if the person making it does not attend to give oral evidence in the proceedings, that its admission or exclusion will result in unfairness to the accused or, if there is more than one, to any of them.

26 Statements in documents that appear to have been prepared for purposes of criminal proceedings or investigations

Where a statement which is admissible in criminal proceedings by virtue of sections 23 or 24 above appears to the court to have been prepared, otherwise than in accordance with section 3 of the Criminal Justice (International Co-operation) Act 1990 or an order under paragraph 6 of Schedule 13 to this Act or under section 30 or 31 below, for the purposes –

(a) of pending or contemplated criminal proceedings; or

(b) of a criminal investigation,

the statement shall not be given in evidence in any criminal proceedings without the leave of the court, and the court shall not give leave unless it is of the opinion that the statement ought to be admitted in the interests of justice; and in considering whether its admission would be in the interests of justice, it shall be the duty of the court to have regard –

(i) to the contents of the statement;

(ii) to any risk, having regard in particular to whether it is likely to be possible to controvert the statement if the person making it does not attend to give oral evidence in the proceedings, that its admission or exclusion will result in unfairness to the accused or, if there is more than one, to any of them; and

(iii) to any other circumstances that appear to the court to be relevant.

This section shall not apply to proceedings before a magistrates' court inquiring into an offence as examing justices.

27 Proof of statements contained in documents

Where a statement contained in a document is admissible as evidence in criminal proceedings, it may be proved –

(a) by the production of that document; or

(b) (whether or not that document is still in existence) by the production of a copy of that document, or of the material part of it,

authenticated in such manner as the court may approve; and it is immaterial for the purposes of this subsection how many removes there are between a copy and the original.

This section shall not apply to proceedings before a magistrates' court inquiring into an offence as examining justices.

28 Documentary evidence – supplementary

(1) Nothing in this Part of this Act shall prejudice –

(a) the admissibility of a statement not made by a person while giving oral evidence in court which is admissible otherwise than by virtue of this Part of this Act; or

(b) any power of a court to exclude at its discretion a statement admissible by virtue of this Part of this Act.

(2) Schedule 2 to this Act shall have effect for the purpose of supplementing this Part of this Act.

PART III

OTHER PROVISIONS ABOUT EVIDENCE IN CRIMINAL PROCEEDINGS

30 Expert reports

(1) An expert report shall be admissible as evidence in criminal proceedings, whether or not the person making it attends to give oral evidence in those proceedings.

(2) If it is proposed that the person making the report shall not give oral evidence, the report shall only be admissible with the leave of the court.

(3) For the purpose of determining whether to give leave the court shall have regard –

(a) to the contents of the report;

(b) to the reasons why it is proposed that the person making the report shall not give oral evidence;

(c) to any risk, having regard in particular to whether it is likely to be possible to controvert statements in the report if the person making it does not attend to give oral evidence in the proceedings, that its admission or exclusion will result in unfairness to other accused or, if there is more than one, to any of them; and

(d) to any other circumstances that appear to the court to be relevant.

(4) An expert report, when admitted, shall be evidence of any fact or opinion of which the person making it could have given oral evidence.

(4A) Where the proceedings mentioned in subsection (1) above are proceedings before a magistrates' court inquiring into an offence as examining justices this section shall have effect with the omission of –

(a) in subsection (1) the words 'whether or not the person making it attends to give oral evidence in those proceedings', and

(b) subsections (2) to (4).

(5) In this section 'expert report' means a written report by a person dealing wholly or mainly with matters on which he is (or would if living be) qualified to give expert evidence.

31 Form of evidence and glossaries

For the purpose of helping members of juries to understand complicated issues of fact or technical terms Crown Court Rules may make provision –

(a) as to the furnishing of evidence in any form, notwithstanding the existence of admissible material from which the evidence to be given in that form would be derived; and

(b) as to the furnishing of glossaries for such purposes as may be specified;

in any case where the court gives leave for, or requires, evidence or a glossary to be so furnished.

32 Evidence through television links

(1) A person other than the accused may give evidence through a live television link in proceedings to which subsection (1A) below applies if –

(a) the witness is outside the United Kingdom; or

(b) the witness is a child, or is to be cross-examined following the admission under section 32A below of a video recording of testimony from him, and the offence is one to which subsection (2) below applies,

but evidence may not be so given without the leave of the court.

(1A) This subsection applies –

(a) to trials on indictment, appeals to the criminal division of the Court of Appeal and hearings of references under section 9 of the Criminal Appeal Act 1995; and

(b) to proceedings in youth courts, appeals to the Crown Court arising out of such proceedings and hearings of references under section 11 of the Criminal Appeal Act 1995 so arising.

(2) This subsection applies –

(a) to an offence which involves an assault on, or injury or a threat of injury to, a person;

(b) to an offence under section 1 of the Children and Young Persons Act 1933 (cruelty to persons under 16);

(c) to an offence under the Sexual Offences Act 1956, the Indecency with Children Act 1960, the Sexual Offences Act 1967, section 54 of the Criminal Law Act 1977 or the Protection of Children Act 1978; and

(d) to an offence which consists of attempting or conspiring to commit, or of aiding, abetting, counselling, procuring or inciting the commission of, an offence falling within paragraph (a), (b) or (c) above.

(3) A statement made on oath by a witness outside the United Kingdom and given in evidence through a television link by virtue of this section shall be treated for the purposes of section 1 of the Perjury Act 1911 as having been made in the proceedings in which it is given in evidence.

(3A) Where, in the case of any proceedings before a youth court –

(a) leave is given by virtue of subsection (1)(b) above for evidence to be given through a television link; and

(b) suitable facilities for receiving such evidence are not available at any petty-sessional court-house in which the court can (apart from this subsection) lawfully sit,

the court may sit for the purposes of the whole or any part of those proceedings at any place at which such facilities are available and which has been appointed for the purposes of this subsection by the justices acting for the petty sessions area for which the court acts.

(3B) A place appointed under subsection (3A) above may be outside the petty sessions area for which it is appointed; but it shall be deemed to be in that area for the purpose of the jurisdiction of the justices acting for that area.

(3C) Where –

(a) the court gives leave for a person to give evidence through a live television link, and

(b) the leave is given by virtue of subsection (1)(b) above,

then, subject to subsection (3D) below, the person concerned may not give evidence otherwise than through a live television link.

(3D) In a case falling within subsection (3C) above the court may give permission for the person to give evidence otherwise than through a live television link if it appears to the court to be in the interests of justice to give such permission.

(3E) Permission may be given under subsection (3D) above –

(a) on an application by a party to the case, or

(b) of the court's own motion;

but no application may be made under paragraph (a) above unless there has been a material change of circumstances since the leave was given by virtue of subsection (1)(b) above.

(4) Without prejudice to the generality of any enactment conferring power to make rules to which this subsection applies, such rules may make such provision as appears to the authority making them to be necessary or expedient for the purposes of this section.

(5) The rules to which subsection (4) above applies are the Magistrates' Courts Rules, Crown Court Rules and Criminal Appeal Rules.

(6) Subsection (7) of section 32A below shall apply for the purposes of this section as it applies for the purposes of that section, but with the omission of the references to a person being, in the cases there mentioned, under the age of fifteen years or under the age of eighteen years.

32A Video recordings of testimony from child witnesses

(1) This section applies in relation to the following proceedings, namely –

(a) trials on indictment for any offence to which section 32(2) above applies;

(b) appeals to the Criminal Division of the Court of Appeal and hearings of references under section 9 of the Criminal Appeal Act 1995 in respect of any such offence; and

(c) proceedings in youth courts for any such offence, appeals to the Crown Court arising out of such proceedings and hearings of references under section 11 of the Criminal Appeal Act 1995 so arising.

(2) In any such proceedings a video recording of an interview which –

(a) is conducted between an adult and a child who is not the accused or one of the accused ('the child witness'); and

(b) relates to any matter in issue in the proceedings,

may, with the leave of the court, be given in evidence in so far as it is not excluded by the court under subsection (3) below.

(3) Where a video recording is tendered in evidence under this section, the court shall (subject to the exercise of any power of the court to exclude evidence which is otherwise admissible) give leave under subsection (2) above unless –

(a) it appears that the child witness will not be available for cross-examination;

(b) any rules of court requiring disclosure of the circumstances in which the recording was made have not been complied with to the satisfaction of the court; or

(c) the court is of the opinion, having regard to all the circumstances of the case, that in the interests of justice the recording ought not to be admitted;

and where the court gives such leave it may, if it is of the opinion that in the interests of justice any part of the recordings ought not to be admitted, direct that that part shall be excluded.

(4) In considering whether any part of a recording ought to be excluded under subsection (3) above, the court shall consider whether any prejudice to the accused, or one of the accused, which might result from the admission of that part is outweighed by the desirability of showing the whole, or substantially the whole, of the recorded interview.

(5) Where a video recording is admitted under this section –

(a) the child witness shall be called by the party who tendered it in evidence;

(b) that witness shall not be examined in chief on any matter which, in the opinion of the court, has been dealt with adequately in his recorded testimony.

(6) Where a video recording is given in evidence under this section, any statement made by the child witness which is disclosed by the recording shall be treated as if given by that witness in direct oral testimony; and accordingly –

(a) any such statement shall be admissible evidence of any fact of which such testimony from him would be admissible;

(b) no such statement shall be capable of corroborating any other evidence given by him;

and in estimating the weight, if any, to be attached to such a statement, regard shall be had to all the circumstances from which any inference can reasonably be drawn (as to its accuracy or otherwise).

(6A) Where the court gives leave under subsection (2) above the child witness shall not give relevant evidence (within the meaning given by subsection (6D) below) otherwise than by means of the video recording; but this is subject to subsection (6B) below.

(6B) In a case falling within subsection (6A) above the court may give permission for the child witness to give relevant evidence (within the meaning given by subsection (6D) below) otherwise than by means of the video recording if it appears to the court to be in the interests of justice to give such permission.

(6C) Permission may be given under subsection (6B) above –

(a) on an application by a party to the case, or

(b) of the court's own motion;

but not application may be made under paragraph (a) above unless there has been a material change of circumstances since the leave was given under subsection (2) above.

(6D) For the purposes of subsections (6A) and (6B) above evidence is relevant evidence if –

(a) it is evidence in chief on behalf of the party who tendered the video recording, and

(b) it relates to matter which, in the opinion of the court, is dealt with in the recording and which the court has not directed to be excluded under subsection (3) above.

(7) In this section 'child' means a person who –

(a) in the case of an offence falling within section 32(2)(a) or (b) above, is under fourteen years of age or, if he was under that age when the video recording was made, is under fifteen years of age; or

(b) in the case of an offence falling within section 32(2)(c) above, is under seventeen years of age or, if he was under that age when the video recording was made, is under eighteen years of age.

(8) Any reference in subsection (7) above to an offence falling within paragraph (a), (b) or (c) of section 32(2) above includes a reference to an offence which consists of attempting or conspiring to commit, or of aiding, abetting, counselling, procuring or inciting the commission of, an offence falling within that paragraph.

(9) In this section –

'statement' includes any representation of fact, whether made in words or otherwise;

'video recording' means any recording, on any medium, from which a moving image may by any means be produced and includes the accompanying sound-track.

(10) A magistrates' court inquiring into an offence as examining justices under section 6 of the Magistrates' Courts Act 1980 may consider any video recording as respects which leave under subsection (2) above is to be sought at the trial.

(11) Without prejudice to the generality of any enactment conferring power to make rules of court, such rules may make such provision as appears to the authority making them to be necessary or expedient for the purposes of this section.

(12) Nothing in this section shall prejudice the admissibility of any video recording which would be admissible apart from this section.

33A Evidence given by children

(1) A child's evidence in criminal proceedings shall be given unsworn.

(2) A deposition of a child's unsworn evidence may be taken for the purposes of criminal proceedings as if that evidence had been given on oath.

(2A) A child's evidence shall be received unless it appears to the court that the child is incapable of giving intelligible testimony.

(3) In this section 'child' means a person under fourteen years of age.

34 Abolition of requirements of corroboration for unsworn evidence of children

(2) Any requirement whereby at a trial on indictment it is obligatory for the court to give the jury a warning about convicting the accused on the uncorroborated evidence of a child is abrogated.

(3) Unsworn evidence admitted by virtue of section 52 of the Criminal Justice Act 1991 may corroborate evidence (sworn or unsworn) given by any other person.

34A Cross-examination of alleged child victims

(1) No person who is charged with an offence to which section 32(2) applies shall cross-examine in person any witness who –

(a) is alleged –

(i) to be a person against whom the offence was committed; or

(ii) to have witnessed the commission of the offence; and

(b) is a child, or is to be cross-examined following the admission under section 32A above of a video recording of testimony from him.

(2) Subsection (7) of section 32A above shall apply for the purposes of this section as it applies for the purposes of that section, but with the omission of the references to a person being, in the cases there mentioned, under the age of fifteen years or under the age of eighteen years.

139 Offence of having article with blade or point in public place

(1) Subject to subsections (4) and (5) below, any person who has an article to which this section applies with him in a public place shall be guilty of an offence.

(2) Subject to subsection (3) below, this section applies to any article which has a blade or is sharply pointed except a folding pocketknife.

(3) This section applies to a folding pocketknife if the cutting edge of its blade exceeds three inches.

(4) It shall be a defence for a person charged with an offence under this section to prove that he had good reason or lawful authority for having the article with him in a public place.

(5) Without prejudice to the generality of subsection (4) above, it shall be a

defence for a person charged with an offence under this section to prove that he had the article with him –

(a) for use at work;

(b) for religious reasons; or

(c) as part of any national costume. ...

139A Offence of having article with blade or point (or offensive weapon) on school premises

(1) Any person who has an article to which section 139 of this Act applies with him on school premises shall be guilty of an offence.

(2) Any person who has an offensive weapon within the meaning of section 1 of the Prevention of Crime Act 1953 with him on school premises shall be guilty of an offence.

(3) It shall be a defence for a person charged with an offence under subsection (1) or (2) above to prove that he had good reason or lawful authority for having the article or weapon with him on the premises in question.

(4) Without prejudice to the generality of subsection (3) above, it shall be a defence for a person charged with an offence under subsection (1) or (2) above to prove that he had the article or weapon in question with him –

(a) for use at work,

(b) for educational purposes,

(c) for religious reasons, or

(d) as part of any national costume. ...

SCHEDULE 2

DOCUMENTARY EVIDENCE – SUPPLEMENTARY

1. Where a statement is admitted as evidence in criminal proceedings by virtue of Part II of this Act –

(a) any evidence which, if the person making the statement had been called as a witness, would have been admissible as relevant to his credibility as a witness shall be admissible for that purpose in those proceedings;

(b) evidence may, with the leave of the court, be given of any matter which, if that person had been called as a witness, could have been put to him in cross-examination as relevant to his credibility as a witness but of which evidence could not have been adduced by the cross-examining party; and

(c) evidence tending to prove that that person, whether before or after making the statement, made (whether orally or not) some other statement which is inconsistent with it shall be admissible for the purpose of showing that he has contradicted himself.

2. A statement which is given in evidence by virtue of Part II of this Act shall not be capable of corroborating evidence given by the person making it.

3. In estimating the weight, if any, to be attached to such a statement regard shall be had to all the circumstances from which any inference can reasonably be drawn as to its accuracy or otherwise.

4. Without prejudice to the generality of any enactment conferring power to make them –

(a) Crown Court Rules;

(b) Criminal Appeal Rules; and

(c) rules under section 144 of the Magistrates' Courts Act 1980,

may make such provision as appears to the authority making any of them to be necessary or expedient for the purposes of Part II of this Act.

5. – (1) In Part II of this Act –

'document' means anything in which information of any description is recorded;

'copy', in relation to a document, means anything onto which information recorded in the document has been copied, by whatever means and whether directly or indirectly; and

'statement' means any representation of fact, however made.

(2) For the purposes of Part II of this Act evidence which, by reason of a defect of speech or hearing, a person called as a witness gives in writing or by signs shall be treated as given orally.

6. In Part II of this Act 'confession' has the meaning assigned to it by section 82 of the Police and Criminal Evidence Act 1984.

As amended by the Criminal Justice (International Co-operation) Act 1990, s31(1), Schedule 4, para 6(1), (2); Criminal Justice Act 1991, ss52(1), 54, 55(2)-(7), 100, 101(2), Schedule 11, para 37, Schedule 13; Criminal Justice and Public Order Act 1994, ss32(2), 50, 168(1), (3), Schedule 9, para 31, 32, Schedule 11; Criminal Appeal Act 1995, s29(1) Schedule 2, para 16(1)–(3); Civil Evidence Act 1995, s15(1), Schedule 1, para 12; Criminal Procedure and Investigations Act 1996, ss47, 62(1)–(3), 80, Schedule 1, Pt II, paras 28–33, Schedule 5(10) (s62(1)–(3) from a day to be appointed); Offensive Weapons Act 1996, s4(1).

COPYRIGHT, DESIGNS AND PATENTS ACT 1988

(1988 c 48)

280 Privilege for communications with patent agents

(1) This section applies to communications as to any matter relating to the protection of any invention, design, technical information or trade mark, or as to any matter involving passing off.

(2) Any such communication –

(a) between a person and his patent agent, or

(b) for the purpose of obtaining, or in response to a request for, information which a person is seeking for the purpose of instructing his patent agent,

is privileged from disclosure in legal proceedings in England, Wales or Northern Ireland in the same way as a communication between a person and his solicitor or, as the case may be, a communication for the purpose of obtaining, or in response to a request for, information which a person seeks for the purpose of instructing his solicitor.

As amended by the Trade Marks Act 1994, s106(1), Schedule 4, para 8(1), (3).

ROAD TRAFFIC OFFENDERS ACT 1988

(1988 c 53)

15 Use of specimens in proceedings for an offence under sections [3A], 4 or 5 of the Road Traffic Act

(1) This section and section 16 of this Act apply in respect of proceedings for an offence under section 3A, 4 or 5 of the Road Traffic Act 1988 (driving offences connected with drink or drugs); and expressions used in this section and section 16 of this Act have the same meaning as in sections 3A to 10 of that Act.

(2) Evidence of the proportion of alcohol or any drug in a specimen of breath, blood or urine provided by the accused shall, in all cases (including cases where the specimen was not provided in connection with the alleged offence), be taken into account and, subject to subsection (3) below, it shall be assumed that the proportion of alcohol in the accused's breath, blood or urine at the time of the alleged offence was not less than in the specimen.

(3) That assumption shall not be made if the accused proves –

(a) that he consumed alcohol before he provided the specimen and –

(i) in relation to an offence under section 3A, after the time of the alleged offence, and

(ii) otherwise, after he had ceased to drive, attempt to drive or be in charge of a vehicle on a road or other public place, and

(b) that had he not done so the proportion of alcohol in his breath, blood or urine would not have exceeded the prescribed limit and, if it is alleged that he was unfit to drive through drink, would not have been such as to impair his ability to drive properly.

(4) A specimen of blood shall be disregarded unless it was taken from the accused with his consent by a medical practitioner.

(5) Where, at the time a specimen of blood or urine was provided by the accused, he asked to be provided with such a specimen, evidence of the proportion of alcohol or any drug found in the specimen is not admissible on behalf of the prosecution unless –

(a) the specimen in which the alcohol or drug was found is one of two parts into which the specimen provided by the accused was divided at the time it was provided, and

(b) the other part was supplied to the accused.

16 Documentary evidence as to specimens in such proceedings

(1) Evidence of the proportion of alcohol or a drug in a specimen of breath, blood or urine may, subject to subsections (3) and (4) below and to section 15(5) of this Act, be given by the production of a document or documents purporting to be whichever of the following is appropriate, that is to say –

(a) a statement automatically produced by the device by which the proportion of alcohol in a specimen of breath was measured and a certificate signed by a constable (which may but need not be contained in the same document as the statement) that the statement relates to a specimen provided by the accused at the date and time shown in the statement, and

(b) a certificate signed by an authorised analyst as to the proportion of alcohol or any drug found in a specimen of blood or urine identified in the certificate.

(2) Subject to subsections (3) and (4) below, evidence that a specimen of blood was taken from the accused with his consent by a medical practitioner may be given by the production of a document purporting to certify that fact and to be signed by a medical practitioner.

(3) Subject to subsection (4) below –

(a) a document purporting to be such a statement or such a certificate (or both such a statement and such a certificate) as is mentioned in subsection (1)(a) above is admissible in evidence on behalf of the prosecution in pursuance of this section only if a copy of it either has been handed to the accused when the document was produced or has been served on him not later than seven days before the hearing, and

(b) any other document is so admissible only if a copy if it has been served on the accused not later than seven days before the hearing.

(4) A document purporting to be a certificate (or so much of a document as purports to be a certificate) is not so admissible if the accused, not later than three days before the hearing or within such further time as the court may in special circumstances allow, has served notice on the prosecutor requiring the attendance at the hearing of the person by whom the document purports to be signed. ...

(6A) Where the proceedings mentioned in section 15(1) of this Act are proceedings before a magistrates' court inquiring into an offence as examining justices this section shall have effect with the omission of subsection (4).

As amended by the Road Traffic Act 1991, s48, Schedule 4, para 87; Criminal Procedure and Investigations Act 1996, s47, Schedule 1, Pt II, para 37.

CHILDREN ACT 1989

(1989 c 41)

7 Welfare reports

(1) A court considering any question with respect to a child under this Act may –

(a) ask a probation officer; or

(b) ask a local authority to arrange for –

(i) an officer of the authority; or

(ii) such other person (other than a probation officer) as the authority considers appropriate,

to report to the court on such matters relating to the welfare of that child as are required to be dealt with in the report.

(2) The Lord Chancellor may make regulations specifying matters which, unless the court orders otherwise, must be dealt with in any report under this section.

(3) The report may be made in writing, or orally, as the court requires.

(4) Regardless of any enactment or rule of law which would otherwise prevent it from doing so, the court may take account of –

(a) any statement contained in the report; and

(b) any evidence given in respect of the matters referred to in the report,

in so far as the statement or evidence is, in the opinion of the court, relevant to the question which it is considering.

(5) It shall be the duty of the authority or probation officer to comply with any request for a report under this section.

31 Care and supervision orders

(9) In this section –

'authorised person' means –

(a) the National Society for the Prevention of Cruelty to Children and any of its officers; and

(b) any person authorised by order of the Secretary of State to bring proceedings under this section and any officer of a body which is so authorised ...

42 Right of guardian ad litem to have access to local authority records

(1) Where a person has been appointed as a guardian ad litem under this Act he shall have the right at all reasonable times to examine and take copies of –

(a) any records of, or held by, a local authority or an authorised person which were compiled in connection with the making, or proposed making, by any person of any application under this Act with respect to the child concerned;

(b) any records of, or held by, a local authority which were compiled in connection with any functions which stand referred to their social services committee under the Local Authority Social Services Act 1970, so far as those records relate to that child; or

(c) any records of, or held by, an authorised person which were compiled in connection with the activities of that person, so far as those records relate to that child.

(2) Where a guardian ad litem takes a copy of any record which he is entitled to examine under this section, that copy or any part of it shall be admissible as evidence of any matter referred to in any –

(a) report which he makes to the court in the proceedings in question; or

(b) evidence which he gives in those proceedings.

(3) Subsection (2) has effect regardless of any enactment or rule of law which would otherwise prevent the record in question being admissible in evidence.

(4) In this section 'authorised person' has the same meaning as in section 31.

96 Evidence given by, or with respect to, children

(1) Subsection (2) applies where a child who is called as a witness in any civil proceedings does not, in the opinion of the court, understand the nature of an oath.

(2) The child's evidence may be heard by the court if, in its opinion –

(a) he understands that it is his duty to speak the truth; and

(b) he has sufficient understanding to justify his evidence being heard.

(3) The Lord Chancellor may by order make provision for the admissibility of evidence which would otherwise be inadmissible under any rule of law relating to hearsay.

(4) An order under subsection (3) may only be made with respect to –

(a) civil proceedings in general or such civil proceedings, or class of civil proceedings, as may be prescribed; and

(b) evidence in connection with the upbringing, maintenance or welfare of a child.

(5) An order under subsection (3) –

(a) may, in particular, provide for the admissibility of statements which are made orally or in a prescribed form or which are recorded by any prescribed method of recording;

(b) may make different provision for different purposes and in relation to different descriptions of court; and

(c) may make such amendments and repeals in any enactment relating to evidence (other than in this Act) as the Lord Chancellor considers necessary or expedient in consequence of the provision made by the order.

(6) Subsection (5)(b) is without prejudice to section 104(4).

(7) In this section –

'civil proceedings' means civil proceedings, before any tribunal, in relation to which the strict rules of evidence apply, whether as a matter of law or by agreement of the parties, and references to 'the court' shall be construed accordingly;

'prescribed' means prescribed by an order under subsection (3).

98 Self-incrimination

(1) In any proceedings in which a court is hearing an application for an order under Part IV [care and supervision] or V [protection of children], no person shall be excused from –

(a) giving evidence on any matter; or

(b) answering any question put to him in the course of his giving evidence,

on the ground that doing so might incriminate him or his spouse of an offence.

(2) A statement or admission made in such proceedings shall not be admissible in evidence against the person making it or his spouse in proceedings for an offence other than perjury.

As amended by the Courts and Legal Services Act 1990, ss116, 125(7), Schedule 16, para 18, Schedule 20; Civil Evidence Act 1995, s15(1), Schedule 1, para 16.

CRIMINAL JUSTICE (INTERNATIONAL CO-OPERATION) ACT 1990

(1990 c 5)

3 Overseas evidence for use in United Kingdom

(1) Where on an application made in accordance with subsection (2) below it appears to a justice of the peace or a judge or, in Scotland, to a sheriff or a judge –

(a) that an offence has been committed or that there are reasonable grounds for suspecting that an offence has been committed; and

(b) that proceedings in respect of the offence have been instituted or that the offence is being investigated,

he may issue a letter ('a letter of request') requesting assistance in obtaining outside the United Kingdom such evidence as is specified in the letter for use in the proceedings or investigation.

(2) An application under subsection (1) above may be made by a prosecuting authority or, if proceedings have been instituted, by the person charged in those proceedings.

(3) A prosecuting authority which is for the time being designated for the purposes of this section by an order made by the Secretary of State by statutory instrument may itself issue a letter of request if –

(a) it is satisfied as to the matters mentioned in subsection (1)(a) above; and

(b) the offence in question is being investigated or the authority has instituted proceedings in respect of it.

(4) Subject to subsection (5) below, a letter of request shall be sent to the Secretary of State for transmission either –

(a) to a court or tribunal specified in the letter and exercising jurisdiction in the place where the evidence is to be obtained; or

(b) to any authority recognised by the government of the country or territory in question as the appropriate authority for receiving requests for assistance of the kind to which this section applies.

(5) In cases of urgency a letter of request may be sent direct to such a court or tribunal as is mentioned in subsection (4)(a) above.

(6) In this section 'evidence' includes documents and other articles.

(7) Evidence obtained by virtue of a letter of request shall not without the consent of such an authority as is mentioned in subsection (4)(b) above be used for any purpose other than that specified in the letter; and when any document or other article obtained pursuance to a letter of request is no longer required for that purpose (or for any other purpose for which such consent has been obtained), it shall be returned to such an authority unless that authority indicates that the document or article need not be returned.

(8) In exercising the discretion conferred by section 25 of the Criminal Justice Act 1988 (exclusion of evidence otherwise admissible) in relation to a statement contained in evidence taken pursuant to a letter of request the court shall have regard –

(a) to whether it was possible to challenge the statement by questioning the person who made it; and

(b) if proceedings have been instituted, to whether the local law allowed the parties to the proceedings to be legally represented when the evidence was being taken.

6 Transfer of overseas prisoner to give evidence or assist investigation in the United Kingdom

(1) This section has effect where –

(a) a witness order has been made or a witness summons or citation issued in criminal proceedings in the United Kingdom in respect of a person ('a prisoner') who is detained in custody in a country or territory outside the United Kingdom by virtue of a sentence or order of a court or tribunal exercising criminal jurisdiction in that country or territory; or

(b) it appears to the Secretary of State that it is desirable for a prisoner to be identified in, or otherwise by his presence to assist, such proceedings or the investigation in the United Kingdom of an offence.

(2) If the Secretary of State is satisfied that the appropriate authority in the country or territory where the prisoner is detained will make arrangements for him to come to the United Kingdom to give evidence pursuant to the witness order, witness summons or citation or, as the case

may be, for the purpose mentioned in subsection (1)(b) above, he may issue a warrant under this section.

(3) No warrant shall be issued under this section in respect of any prisoner unless he has consented to being brought to the United Kingdom to give evidence as aforesaid or, as the case may be, for the purpose mentioned in subsection (1)(b) above but a consent once given shall not be capable of being withdrawn after the issue of the warrant.

(4) The effect of the warrant shall be to authorise –

(a) the bringing of the prisoner to the United Kingdom;

(b) the taking of the prisoner to, and his detention in custody at, such place or places in the United Kingdom as are specified in the warrant; and

(c) the returning of the prisoner to the country or territory from which he has come.

(5) Subsections (4) to (8) of section 5 above shall have effect in relation to a warrant issued under this section as they have effect in relation to a warrant issued under that section.

(6) A person shall not be subject to the Immigration Act 1971 in respect of his entry into or presence in the United Kingdom in pursuance of a warrant under this section but if the warrant ceases to have effect while he is still in the United Kingdom –

(a) he shall be treated for the purposes of that Act as if he has then illegally entered the United Kingdom; and

(b) the provisions of Schedule 2 to that Act shall have effect accordingly except that paragraph 20(1) (liability of carrier for expenses of custody, etc of illegal entrant) shall not have effect in relation to directions for his removal given by virtue of this subsection.

(7) This section applies to a person detained in custody in a country or territory outside the United Kingdom in consequence of having been transferred there –

(a) from the United Kingdom under the Repatriation of Prisoners Act 1984; or

(b) under any similar provision or arrangement from any other country or territory,

as it applies to a person detained as mentioned in subsection (1) above.

COURTS AND LEGAL SERVICES ACT 1990

(1990 c 41)

5 Witness statements

(1) Rules of court may make provision –

(a) requiring, in specified circumstances, any party to civil proceedings to serve on the other parties a written statement of the oral evidence which he intends to adduce on any issue of fact to be decided at the trial;

(b) enabling the court to direct any party to civil proceedings to serve such a statement on the other party; and

(c) prohibiting a party who fails to comply with such a requirement or direction from adducing oral evidence on the issue of fact to which it relates.

(2) Where a party to proceedings has refused to comply with such a requirement or direction, the fact that his refusal was on the ground that the required statement would have been a document which was privileged from disclosure shall not affect any prohibition imposed by virtue of subsection (1)(c).

(3) This section is not to be read as prejudicing in any way any other powers to make rules of court.

63 Legal professional privilege

(1) This section applies to any communication made to or by a person who is not a barrister or solicitor at any time when that person is –

(a) providing advocacy or litigation services as an authorised advocate or authorised litigator;

(b) providing conveyancing services as an authorised practitioner; or

(c) providing probate services as a probate practitioner.

(2) Any such communication shall in any legal proceedings be privileged

from disclosure in like manner as if the person in question had at all material times been acting as his client's solicitor.

(3) In subsection (1), 'probate practitioner' means a person to whom section 23(1) of the Solicitors Act 1974 (unqualified person not to prepare probate papers, etc) does not apply.

CHARITIES ACT 1992
(1992 c 41)

63 False statements relating to institutions which are not registered charities

(1) Where

(a) a person solicits money or other property for the benefit of an institution in assocation with a representation that the institution is a registered charity, and

(b) the institution is not such a charity,

he shall be guilty of an offence and liable on summary conviction to a fine not exceeding the fifth level on the standard scale.

(1A) In any proceedings for an offence under subsection (1), it shall be a defence for the accused to prove that he believed on reasonable grounds that the institution was a registered charity.

(2) In this section 'registered charity' means a charity which is for the time being registered in the register of charities kept under section 3 of the Charities Act 1993.

As amended by the Charities Act 1993, s98(1), Schedule 6, para 29(1), (6); Deregulation and Contracting Out Act 1994, s26

FINANCE ACT 1993

(1993 c 34)

204 Method of denoting stamp duty ...

(3) Regulations under this section may provide that where stamp duty is denoted by a method which (in the case of the instrument concerned) is required or permitted by the law in force at the time it is stamped, for the purposes of section 14(4) of the Stamp Act 1891 (instruments not to be given in evidence etc unless stamped in accordance with the law in force at the time of first execution) the method shall be treated as being in accordance with the law in force at the time when the instrument was first executed ...

WELSH LANGUAGE ACT 1993

(1993 c 38)

22 Use of Welsh in legal proceedings

(1) In any legal proceedings in Wales the Welsh language may be spoken by any party, witness or other person who desires to use it, subject in the case of proceedings in a court other than a magistrates' court to such prior notice as may be required by rules of court; and any necessary provision for interpretation shall be made accordingly.

(2) Any power to make rules of court includes power to make provision as to the use, in proceedings in or having a connection with Wales, of documents in the Welsh language.

23 Oaths and affirmations

The Lord Chancellor may make rules prescribing a translation in the Welsh language of any form for the time being prescribed by law as the form of any oath or affirmation to be administered and taken or made in any court in Wales and the translation prescribed by such rules shall, without interpretation, be of the like effect as if it had been administered and taken or made in the English language

CRIMINAL JUSTICE AND PUBLIC ORDER ACT 1994

(1994 c 33)

PART III

COURSE OF JUSTICE: EVIDENCE, PROCEDURE, ETC

32 Abolition of corroboration rules

(1) Any requirement whereby at a trial on indictment it is obligatory for the court to give the jury a warning about convicting the accused on the uncorroborated evidence of a person merely because that person is –

(a) an alleged accomplice of the accused, or

(b) where the offence charged is a sexual offence, the person in respect of whom it is alleged to have been committed,

is hereby abrogated …

(3) Any requirement that –

(a) is applicable at the summary trial of a person for an offence, and

(b) corresponds to the requirement mentioned in subsection (1) above or that mentioned in section 34(2) of the Criminal Justice Act 1988,

is hereby abrogated.

(4) Nothing in this section applies in relation to –

(a) any trial, or

(b) any proceedings before a magistrates' court as examining justices,

which began before the commencement of this section.

33 Abolition of corroboration requirements under Sexual Offences Act 1956

(1) The following provisions of the Sexual Offences Act 1956 (which provide

that a person shall not be convicted of the offence concerned on the evidence of one witness only unless the witness is corroborated) are hereby repealed –

(a) section 2(2) (procurement of woman by threats),

(b) section 3(2) (procurement of woman by false pretences),

(c) section 4(2) (administering drugs to obtain or facilitate intercourse),

(d) section 22(2) (causing prostitution of women), and

(e) section 23(2) (procuration of girl under twenty-one).

(2) Nothing in this section applies in relation to –

(a) any trial, or

(b) any proceedings before a magistrates' court as examining justices,

which began before the commencement of this section.

34 Effect of accused's failure to mention facts when questioned or charged

(1) Where, in any proceedings against a person for an offence, evidence is given that the accused –

(a) at any time before he was charged with the offence, on being questioned under caution by a constable trying to discover whether or by whom the offence had been committed, failed to mention any fact relied on in his defence in those proceedings; or

(b) on being charged with the offence or officially informed that he might be prosecuted for it, failed to mention any such fact,

being a fact which in the circumstances existing at the time the accused could reasonably have been expected to mention when so questioned, charged or informed, as the case may be, subsection (2) below applies.

(2) Where this subsection applies –

(a) a magistrates' court, inquiring into the offence as examining justices;

(b) a judge, in deciding whether to grant an application made by the accused under –

(i) section 6 of the Criminal Justice Act 1987 (application for dismissal of charge of serious fraud in respect of which notice of transfer has been given under section 4 of that Act); or

(ii) paragraph 5 of Schedule 6 to the Criminal Justice Act 1991 (application for dismissal of charge of violent or sexual offence involving child in respect of which notice of transfer has been given under section 53 of that Act);

(c) the court, in determining whether there is a case to answer; and

(d) the court or jury, in determining whether the accused is guilty of the offence charged,

may draw such inferences from the failure as appear proper.

(3) Subject to any directions by the court, evidence tending to establish the failure may be given before or after evidence tending to establish the fact which the accused is alleged to have failed to mention.

(4) This section applies in relation to questioning by persons (other than constables) charged with the duty of investigating offences or charging offenders as it applies in relation to questioning by constables; and in subsection (1) above 'officially informed' means informed by a constable or any such person.

(5) This section does not –

(a) prejudice the admissibility in evidence of the silence or other reaction of the accused in the face of anything said in his presence relating to the conduct in respect of which he is charged, in so far as evidence thereof would be admissible apart from this section; or

(b) preclude the drawing of any inference from any such silence or other reaction of the accused which could properly be drawn apart from this section.

(6) This section does not apply in relation to a failure to mention a fact if the failure occurred before the commencement of this section.

35 Effect of accused's silence at trial

(1) At the trial of any person who has attained the age of fourteen years for an offence, subsections (2) and (3) below apply unless –

(a) the accused's guilt is not in issue; or

(b) it appears to the court that the physical or mental condition of the accused makes it undesirable for him to give evidence;

but subsection (2) below does not apply if, at the conclusion of the evidence for the prosecution, his legal representative informs the court that the accused will give evidence or, where he is unrepresented, the court ascertains from him that he will give evidence.

(2) Where this subsection applies, the court shall, at the conclusion of the evidence for the prosecution, satisfy itself (in the case of proceedings on indictment, in the presence of the jury) that the accused is aware that the

stage has been reached at which evidence can be given for the defence and that he can, if he wishes, give evidence and that, if he chooses not to give evidence, or having been sworn, without good cause refuses to answer any question, it will be permissible for the court or jury to draw such inferences as appear proper from his failure to give evidence or his refusal, without good cause, to answer any question.

(3) Where this subsection applies, the court or jury, in determining whether the accused is guilty of the offence charged, may draw such inferences as appear proper from the failure of the accused to give evidence or his refusal, without good cause, to answer any question.

(4) This section does not render the accused compellable to give evidence on his own behalf, and he shall accordingly not be guilty of contempt of court by reason of a failure to do so.

(5) For the purposes of this section a person who, having been sworn, refuses to answer any question shall be taken to do so without good cause unless –

(a) he is entitled to refuse to answer the question by virtue of any enactment, whenever passed or made, or on the ground of privilege; or

(b) the court in the exercise of its general discretion excuses him from answering it.

(6) Where the age of any person is material for the purposes of subsection (1) above, his age shall for those purposes be taken to be that which appears to the court to be his age.

(7) This section applies –

(a) in relation to proceedings on indictment for an offence, only if the person charged with the offence is arraigned on or after the commencement of this section;

(b) in relation to proceedings in a magistrates' court, only if the time when the court begins to receive evidence in the proceedings falls after the commencement of this section.

36 Effect of accused's failure or refusal to account for objects, substances or marks

(1) Where –

(a) a person is arrested by a constable, and there is –

(i) on his person; or

(ii) in or on his clothing or footwear; or

(iii) otherwise in his possession; or

(iv) in any place in which he is at the time of his arrest,

any object, substance or mark, or there is any mark on any such object; and

(b) that or another constable investigating the case reasonably believes that the presence of the object, substance or mark may be attributable to the participation of the person arrested in the commission of an offence specified by the constable; and

(c) the constable informs the person arrested that he so believes, and requests him to account for the presence of the object, substance or mark; and

(d) the person fails or refuses to do so,

then if, in any proceedings against the person for the offence so specified, evidence of those matters is given, subsection (2) below applies.

(2) Where this subsection applies –

(a) a magistrates' court inquiring into the offence as examining justices;

(b) a judge, in deciding whether to grant an application made by the accused under –

(i) section 6 of the Criminal Justice Act 1987 (application for dismissal of charge of serious fraud in respect of which notice of transfer has been given under section 4 of that Act); or

(ii) paragraph 5 of Schedule 6 to the Criminal Justice Act 1991 (application for dismissal of charge of violent or sexual offence involving child in respect of which notice of transfer has been given under section 53 of that Act);

(c) the court, in determining whether there is a case to answer; and

(d) the court or jury, in determining whether the accused is guilty of the offence charged,

may draw such inferences from the failure or refusal as appear proper.

(3) Subsections (1) and (2) above apply to the condition of clothing or footwear as they apply to a substance or mark theron.

(4) Subsections (1) and (2) above do not apply unless the accused was told in ordinary language by the constable when making the request mentioned in subsection (1)(c) above what the effect of this section would be if he failed or refused to comply with the request.

(5) This section applies in relation to officers of customs and excise as it applies in relation to constables.

(6) This section does not preclude the drawing of any inference from a failure or refusal of the accused to account for the presence of an object, substance or mark or from the condition of clothing or footwear which could properly be drawn apart from this section.

(7) This section does not apply in relation to a failure or refusal which occurred before the commencement of this section.

37 Effect of accused's failure or refusal to account for presence at a particular place

(1) Where –

(a) a person arrested by a constable was found by him at a place at or about the time the offence for which he was arrested is alleged to have been committed; and

(b) that or another constable investigating the offence reasonably believes that the presence of the person at that place and at that time may be attributable to his participation in the commission of the offence; and

(c) the constable informs the person that he so believes, and requests him to account for that presence; and

(d) the person fails or refuses to do so,

then if, in any proceedings against the person for the offence, evidence of those matters is given, subsection (2) below applies.

(2) Where this subsection applies –

(a) a magistrates' court inquiring into the offence as examining justices;

(b) a judge, in deciding whether to grant an application made by the accused under –

(i) section 6 of the Criminal Justice Act 1987 (application for dismissal of charge of serious fraud in respect of which notice of transfer has been given under section 4 of that Act); or

(ii) paragraph 5 of Schedule 6 to the Criminal Justice Act 1991 (application for dismissal of charge of violent or sexual offence involving child in respect of which notice of transfer has been given under section 53 of that Act);

(c) the court, in determining whether there is a case to answer; and

(d) the court or jury, in determining whether the accused is guilty of the offence charged,

may draw such inferences from the failure or refusal as appear proper.

(3) Subsections (1) and (2) do not apply unless the accused was told in ordinary language by the constable when making the request mentioned in subsection (1)(c) above what the effect of this section would be if he failed or refused to comply with the request.

(4) This section applies in relation to officers of customs and excise as it applies in relation to constables.

(5) This section does not preclude the drawing of any inference from a failure or refusal of the accused to account for his presence at a place which could properly be drawn apart from this section.

(6) This section does not apply in relation to a failure or refusal which occurred before the commencement of this section.

38 Interpretation and savings for sections 34, 35, 36 and 37

(1) In sections 34, 35, 36 and 37 of this Act –

'legal representative' means an authorised advocate or authorised litigator, as defined by section 119(1) of the Courts and Legal Services Act 1990; and

'place' includes any building or part of a building, any vehicle, vessel, aircraft or hovercraft and any other place whatsoever.

(2) In sections 34(2), 35(3), 36(2) and 37(2), references to an offence charged include references to any other offence of which the accused could lawfully be convicted on that charge.

(3) A person shall not have the proceedings against him transferred to the Crown Court for trial, have a case to answer or be convicted of an offence solely on an inference drawn from such a failure or refusal as is mentioned in section 34(2), 35(3), 36(2) or 37(2).

(4) A judge shall not refuse to grant such an application as is mentioned in section 34(2)(b), 36(2)(b) and 37(2)(b) solely on an inference drawn from such a failure as is mentioned in section 34(2), 36(2) or 37(2).

(5) Nothing in sections 34, 35, 36 or 37 prejudices the operation of a provision of any enactment which provides (in whatever words) that any answer or evidence given by a person in specified circumstances shall not be

admissible in evidence against him or some other person in any proceedings or class of proceedings (however described, and whether civil or criminal).

In this subsection, the reference to giving evidence is a reference to giving evidence in any manner, whether by furnishing information, making discovery, producing documents or otherwise.

(6) Nothing in sections 34, 35, 36 or 37 prejudices any power of a court, in any proceedings, to exclude evidence (whether by preventing questions being put or otherwise) at its discretion.

As amended by the Criminal Procedure and Investigations Act 1996, ss44(1), (3), (4), (7), 80, Schedule 5(1).

CIVIL EVIDENCE ACT 1995

(1995 c 38)

1 Admissibility of hearsay evidence

(1) In civil proceedings evidence shall not be excluded on the ground that it is hearsay.

(2) In this Act –

(a) 'hearsay' means a statement made otherwise than by a person while giving oral evidence in the proceedings which is tendered as evidence of the matters stated; and

(b) references to hearsay include hearsay of whatever degree.

(3) Nothing in this Act affects the admissibility of evidence admissible apart from this section.

(4) The provisions of sections 2 to 6 (safeguards and supplementary provisions relating to hearsay evidence) do not apply in relation to hearsay evidence admissible apart from this section, notwithstanding that it may also be admissible by virtue of this section.

2 Notice of proposal to adduce hearsay evidence

(1) A party proposing to adduce hearsay evidence in civil proceedings shall, subject to the following provisions of this section, give to the other party or parties to the proceedings –

(a) such notice (if any) of that fact, and

(b) on request, such particulars of or relating to the evidence,

as is reasonable and practicable in the circumstances for the purpose of enabling him or them to deal with any matters arising from its being hearsay.

(2) Provision may be made by rules of court –

(a) specifying classes of proceedings or evidence in relation to which subsection (1) does not apply, and

(b) as to the manner in which (including the time within which) the duties imposed by that subsection are to be complied with in the cases where it does apply.

(3) Subsection (1) may also be excluded by agreement of the parties; and compliance with the duty to give notice may in any case be waived by the person to whom notice is required to be given.

(4) A failure to comply with subsection (1), or with rules under subsection (2)(b), does not affect the admissibility of the evidence but may be taken into account by the court –

(a) in considering the exercise of its powers with respect to the course of proceedings and costs, and

(b) as a matter adversely affecting the weight to be given to the evidence in accordance with section 4.

3 Power to call witness for cross-examination on hearsay statement

Rules of court may provide that where a party to civil proceedings adduces hearsay evidence of a statement made by a person and does not call that person as a witness, any other party to the proceedings may, with the leave of the court, call that person as a witness and cross-examine him on the statement as if he had been called by the first-mentioned party and as if the hearsay statement were his evidence in chief.

4 Considerations relevant to weighing of hearsay evidence

(1) In estimating the weight (if any) to be given to hearsay evidence in civil proceedings the court shall have regard to any circumstances from which any inference can reasonably be drawn as to the reliability or otherwise of the evidence.

(2) Regard may be had, in particular, to the following –

(a) whether it would have been reasonable and practicable for the party by whom the evidence was adduced to have produced the maker of the original statement as a witness;

(b) whether the original statement was made contemporaneously with the occurrence or existence of the matters stated;

(c) whether the evidence involves multiple hearsay;

(d) whether any person involved had any motive to conceal or misrepresent matters;

(e) whether the original statement was an edited account, or was made in collaboration with another or for a particular purpose;

(f) whether the circumstances in which the evidence is adduced as hearsay are such as to suggest an attempt to prevent proper evaluation of its weight.

5 Competence and credibility

(1) Hearsay evidence shall not be admitted in civil proceedings if or to the extent that it is shown to consist of, or to be proved by means of, a statement made by a person who at the time he made the statement was not competent as a witness. For this purpose 'not competent as a witness' means suffering from such mental or physical infirmity, or lack of understanding, as would render a person incompetent as a witness in civil proceedings; but a child shall be treated as competent as a witness if he satisfies the requirements of section 96(2)(a) and (b) of the Children Act 1989 (conditions for reception of unsworn evidence of child).

(2) Where in civil proceedings hearsay evidence is adduced and the maker of the original statement, or of any statement relied upon to prove another statement, is not called as a witness –

(a) evidence which if he had been so called would be admissible for the purpose of attacking or supporting his credibility as a witness is admissible for that purpose in the proceedings; and

(b) evidence tending to prove that, whether before or after he made the statement, he made any other statement inconsistent with it is admissible for the purpose of showing that he had contradicted himself.

Provided that evidence may not be given of any matter of which, if he had been called as a witness and had denied that matter in cross-examination, evidence could not have been adduced by the cross-examining party.

6 Previous statements of witnesses

(1) Subject as follows, the provisions of this Act as to hearsay evidence in civil proceedings apply equally (but with any necessary modifications) in relation to a previous statement made by a person called as a witness in the proceedings.

(2) A party who has called or intends to call a person as a witness in civil proceedings may not in those proceedings adduce evidence of a previous statement made by that person, except –

(a) with the leave of the court, or

(b) for the purpose of rebutting a suggestion that his evidence has been fabricated.

This shall not be construed as preventing a witness statement (that is, a written statement of oral evidence which a party to the proceedings intends to lead) from being adopted by a witness in giving evidence or treated as his evidence.

(3) Where in the case of civil proceedings section 3, 4 or 5 of the Criminal Procedure Act 1865 applies, which make provision as to –

(a) how far a witness may be discredited by the party producing him,

(b) the proof of contradictory statements made by a witness, and

(c) cross-examination as to previous statements in writing,

this Act does not authorise the adducing of evidence of a previous inconsistent or contradictory statement otherwise than in accordance with those sections. This is without prejudice to any provision made by rules of court under section 3 above (power to call witness for cross-examination on hearsay statement).

(4) Nothing in this Act affects any of the rules of law as to the circumstances in which, where a person called as a witness in civil proceedings is cross-examined on a document used by him to refresh his memory, that document may be made evidence in the proceedings.

(5) Nothing in this section shall be construed as preventing a statement of any description referred to above from being admissible by virtue of section 1 as evidence of the matters stated.

7 Evidence formerly admissible at common law

(1) The common law rule effectively preserved by section 9(1) and (2)(a) of the Civil Evidence Act 1968 (admissibility of admissions adverse to a party) is superseded by the provisions of this Act.

(2) The common law rules effectively preserved by section 9(1) and (2)(b) to (d) of the Civil Evidence Act 1968, that is, any rule of law whereby in civil proceedings –

(a) published works dealing with matters of a public nature (for example, histories, scientific works, dictionaries and maps) are admissible as evidence of facts of a public nature stated in them,

(b) public documents (for example, public registers, and returns made under public authority with respect to matters of public interest) are admissible as evidence of facts stated in them, or

(c) records (for example, the records of certain courts, treaties, Crown grants, pardons and commissions) are admissible as evidence of facts stated in them,

shall continue to have effect.

(3) The common law rules effectively preserved by section 9(3) and (4) of the Civil Evidence Act 1968, that is, any rule of law whereby in civil proceedings –

(a) evidence of a person's reputation is admissible for the purpose of proving his good or bad character, or

(b) evidence of reputation or family tradition is admissible –

(i) for the purpose of proving or disproving pedigree or the existence of a marriage, or

(ii) for the purpose of proving or disproving the existence of any public or general right or of identifying any person or thing,

shall continue to have effect in so far as they authorise the court to treat such evidence as proving or disproving that matter. Where any such rule applies, reputation or family tradition shall be treated for the purposes of this Act as a fact and not as a statement or multiplicity of statements about the matter in question.

(4) The words in which a rule of law mentioned in this section is described are intended only to identify the rule and shall not be construed as altering it in any way.

8 Proof of statements contained in documents

(1) Where a statement contained in a document is admissible as evidence in civil proceedings, it may be proved –

(a) by the production of that document, or

(b) whether or not that document is still in existence, by the production of a copy of that document or of the material part of it,

authenticated in such manner as the court may approve.

(2) It is immaterial for this purpose how many removes there are between a copy and the original.

9 Proof of records of business or public authority

(1) A document which is shown to form part of the records of a business or

public authority may be received in evidence in civil proceedings without further proof.

(2) A document shall be taken to form part of the records of a business or public authority if there is produced to the court a certificate to that effect signed by an officer of the business or authority to which the records belong.

For this purpose –

(a) a document purporting to be a certificate signed by an officer of a business or public authority shall be deemed to have been duly given by such an officer and signed by him; and

(b) a certificate shall be treated as signed by a person if it purports to bear a facsimile of his signature.

(3) The absence of an entry in the records of a business or public authority may be proved in civil proceedings by affidavit of an officer of the business or authority to which the records belong.

(4) In this section –

'records' means records in whatever form;

'business' includes any activity regularly carried on over a period of time, whether for profit or not, by any body (whether corporate or not) or by an individual;

'officer' includes any person occupying a responsible position in relation to the relevant activities of the business or public authority or in relation to its records; and

'public authority' includes any public or statutory undertaking, any government department and any person holding office under Her Majesty.

(5) The court may, having regard to the circumstances of the case, direct that all or any of the above provisions of this section do not apply in relation to a particular document or record, or description of documents or records.

10 Admissibility and proof of Ogden Tables

(1) The actuarial tables (together with explanatory notes) for use in personal injury and fatal accident cases issued from time to time by the Government Actuary's Department are admissible in evidence for the purpose of assessing, in an action for personal injury, the sum to be awarded as general damages for future pecuniary loss.

(2) They may be proved by the production of a copy published by Her Majesty's Stationery Office.

(3) For the purposes of this section –

(a) 'personal injury' includes any disease and any impairment of a person's physical or mental condition; and

(b) 'action for personal injury' includes an action brought by virtue of the Law Reform (Miscellaneous Provisions) Act 1934 or the Fatal Accidents Act 1976.

11 Meaning of 'civil proceedings'

In this Act 'civil proceedings' means civil proceedings, before any tribunal, in relation to which the strict rules of evidence apply, whether as a matter of law or by agreement of the parties. References to 'the court' and 'rules of court' shall be construed accordingly.

12 Provisions as to rules of court

(1) Any power to make rules of court regulating the practice or procedure of the court in relation to civil proceedings includes power to make such provision as may be necessary or expedient for carrying into effect the provisions of this Act.

(2) Any rules of court made for the purposes of this Act as it applies in relation to proceedings in the High Court apply, except in so far as their operation is excluded by agreement, to arbitration proceedings to which this Act applies, subject to such modifications as may be appropriate. Any question arising as to what modifications are appropriate shall be determined, in default of agreement, by the arbitrator or umpire, as the case may be.

13 Interpretation

In this Act –

'civil proceedings' has the meaning given by section 11 and 'court' and 'rules of court' shall be construed in accordance with that section;

'document' means anything in which information of any description is recorded, and 'copy', in relation to a document, means anything onto which information recorded in the document has been copied, by whatever means and whether directly or indirectly;

'hearsay' shall be construed in accordance with section 1(2);

'oral evidence' includes evidence which, by reason of a defect of speech or hearing, a person called as a witness gives in writing or by signs;

'the original statement', in relation to hearsay evidence, means the underlying statement (if any) by –

(a) in the case of evidence of fact, a person having personal knowledge of that fact, or

(b) in the case of evidence of opinion, the person whose opinion it is; and

'statement' means any representation of fact or opinion, however made.

14 Savings

(1) Nothing in this Act affects the exclusion of evidence on grounds other than that it is hearsay.

This applies whether the evidence falls to be excluded in pursuance of any enactment or rule of law, for failure to comply with rules of court or an order of the court, or otherwise.

(2) Nothing in this Act affects the proof of documents by means other than those specified in section 8 or 9.

(3) Nothing in this Act affects the operation of the following enactments –

(a) section 2 of the Documentary Evidence Act 1868 (mode of proving certain official documents);

(b) section 2 of the Documentary Evidence Act 1882 (documents printed under the superintendence of Stationery Office);

(c) section 1 of the Evidence (Colonial Statutes) Act 1907 (proof of statutes of certain legislatures);

(d) section 1 of the Evidence (Foreign, Dominion and Colonial Documents) Act 1933 (proof and effect of registers and official certificates of certain countries);

(e) section 5 of the Oaths and Evidence (Overseas Authorities and Countries) Act 1963 (provision in respect of public registers of other countries).

16 Short title, commencement and extent ...

(2) The provisions of this Act come into force on such day as the Lord Chancellor may appoint by order made by statutory instrument, and different days may be appointed for different provisions and for different purposes. ...

NB This Act (except s10) came into force on 31 January 1997.

POLICE ACT 1996
(1996 c 16)

101 Interpretation ...

(2) In this Act 'police purposes', in relation to a police areas, includes the purposes of –

(a) special constables appointed for that area,

(b) police cadets undergoing training with a view to becoming members of the police force maintained for that area, and

(c) civilians employed for the purposes of that force or of any such special constables or cadets.

CRIMINAL PROCEDURE AND INVESTIGATIONS ACT 1996

(1996 c 25)

PART I

DISCLOSURE

1 Application of this Part

(1) This Part applies where –

(a) a person is charged with a summary offence in respect of which a court proceeds to summary trial and in respect of which he pleads not guilty,

(b) a person who has attained the age of 18 is charged with an offence which is triable either way, in respect of which a court proceeds to summary trial and in respect of which he pleads not guilty, or

(c) a person under the age of 18 is charged with an indictable offence in respect of which a court proceeds to summary trial and in respect of which he pleads not guilty.

(2) This Part also applies where –

(a) a person is charged with an indictable offence and he is committed for trial for the offence concerned,

(b) a person is charged with an indictable offence and proceedings for the trial of the person on the charge concerned are transferred to the Crown Court by virtue of a notice of transfer given under section 4 of the Criminal Justice Act 1987 (serious or complex fraud),

(c) a person is charged with an indictable offence and proceedings for the trial of the person on the charge concerned are transferred to the Crown Court by virtue of a notice of transfer served on a magistrates' court under section 53 of the Criminal Justice Act 1991 (certain cases involving children),

(d) a count charging a person with a summary offence is included in an indictment under the authority of section 40 of the Criminal Justice Act 1988 (common assault etc), or

(e) a bill of indictment charging a person with an indictable offence is preferred under the authority of section 2(2)(b) of the Administration of Justice (Miscellaneous Provisions) Act 1933 (bill preferred by direction of Court of Appeal, or by direction or with consent of a judge).

(3) This Part applies in relation to alleged offences into which no criminal investigation has begun before the appointed day.

(4) For the purposes of this section a criminal investigation is an investigation which police officers or other persons have a duty to conduct with a view to it being ascertained –

(a) whether a person should be charged with an offence, or

(b) whether a person charged with an offence is guilty of it.

(5) The reference in subsection (3) to the appointed day is to such day as is appointed for the purposes of this Part by the Secretary of State by order.

2 General interpretation

(1) References to the accused are to the person mentioned in section 1(1) or (2).

(2) Where there is more than one accused in any proceedings this Part applies separately in relation to each of the accused.

(3) References to the prosecutor are to any person acting as prosecutor, whether an individual or a body.

(4) References to material are to material of all kinds, and in particular include references to –

(a) information, and

(b) objects of all descriptions.

(5) References to recording information are to putting it in a durable or retrievable form (such as writing or tape).

(6) This section applies for the purposes of this Part.

3 Primary disclosure by prosecutor

(1) The prosecutor must –

(a) disclose to the accused any prosecution material which has not previously been disclosed to the accused and which in the prosecutor's opinion might undermine the case for the prosecution against the accused, or

(b) give to the accused a written statement that there is no material of a description mentioned in paragraph (a).

(2) For the purposes of this section prosecution material is material –

(a) which is in the prosecutor's possession, and came into his possession in connection with the case for the prosecution against the accused, or

(b) which, in pursuance of a code operative under Part II, he has inspected in connection with the case for the prosecution against the accused.

(3) Where material consists of information which has been recorded in any form the prosecutor discloses it for the purposes of this section –

(a) by securing that a copy is made of it and that the copy is given to the accused, or

(b) if in the prosecutor's opinion that is not practicable or not desirable, by allowing the accused to inspect it at a reasonable time and a reasonable place or by taking steps to secure that he is allowed to do so;

and a copy may be in such a form as the prosecutor thinks fit and need not be in the same form as that in which the information has already been recorded.

(4) Where material consists of information which has not been recorded the prosecutor discloses it for the purposes of this section by securing that it is recorded in such form as he thinks fit and –

(a) by securing that a copy is made of it and that the copy is given to the accused, or

(b) if in the prosecutor's opinion that is not practicable or not desirable, by allowing the accused to inspect it at a reasonable time and a reasonable place or by taking steps to secure that he is allowed to do so.

(5) Where material does not consist of information the prosecutor discloses it for the purposes of this section by allowing the accused to inspect it at a reasonable time and a reasonable place or by taking steps to secure that he is allowed to do so.

(6) Material must not be disclosed under this section to the extent that the court, on an application by the prosecutor, concludes it is not in the public interest to disclose it and orders accordingly.

(7) Material must not be disclosed under this section to the extent that –

(a) it has been intercepted in obedience to a warrant issued under section 2 of the Interception of Communications Act 1985, or

(b) it indicates that such a warrant has been issued or that material has been intercepted in obedience to such a warrant.

(8) The prosecutor must act under this section during the period which, by virtue of section 12, is the relevant period for this section.

4 Primary disclosure: further provisions

(1) This section applies where –

(a) the prosecutor acts under section 3, and

(b) before so doing he was given a document in pursuance of provision included, by virtue of section 24(3), in a code operative under Part II.

(2) In such a case the prosecutor must give the document to the accused at the same time as the prosecutor acts under section 3.

5 Compulsory disclosure by accused

(1) Subject to subsections (2) to (4), this section applies where –

(a) this Part applies by virtue of section 1(2), and

(b) the prosecutor complies with section 3 or purports to comply with it.

(2) Where this Part applies by virtue of section 1(2)(b), this section does not apply unless –

(a) a copy of the notice of transfer, and

(b) copies of the documents containing the evidence,

have been given to the accused under regulations made under section 5(9) of the Criminal Justice Act 1987.

(3) Where this Part applies by virtue of section 1(2)(c), this section does not apply unless –

(a) a copy of the notice of transfer, and

(b) copies of the documents containing the evidence,

have been given to the accused under regulations made under paragraph 4 of Schedule 6 to the Criminal Justice Act 1991.

(4) Where this Part applies by virtue of section 1(2)(e), this section does not apply unless the prosecutor has served on the accused a copy of the indictment and a copy of the set of documents containing the evidence which is the basis of the charge.

(5) Where this section applies, the accused must give a defence statement to the court and the prosecutor.

(6) For the purposes of this section a defence statement is a written statement –

(a) setting out in general terms the nature of the accused's defence,

(b) indicating the matters on which he takes issue with the prosecution, and

(c) setting out, in the case of each such matter, the reason why he takes issue with the prosecution.

(7) If the defence statement discloses an alibi the accused must give particulars of the alibi in the statement, including –

(a) the name and address of any witness the accused believes is able to give evidence in support of the alibi, if the name and address are known to the accused when the statement is given;

(b) any information in the accused's possession which might be of material assistance in finding any such witness, if his name or address is not known to the accused when the statement is given.

(8) For the purposes of this section evidence in support of an alibi is evidence tending to show that by reason of the presence of the accused at a particular place or in a particular area at a particular time he was not, or was unlikely to have been, at the place where the offence is alleged to have been committed at the time of its alleged commission.

(9) The accused must give a defence statement under this section during the period which, by virtue of section 12, is the relevant period for this section.

6 Voluntary disclosure by accused

(1) This section applies where –

(a) this Part applies by virtue of section 1(1), and

(b) the prosecutor complies with section 3 or purports to comply with it.

(2) The accused –

(a) may give a defence statement to the prosecutor, and

(b) if he does so, must also give such a statement to the court.

(3) Subsections (6) to (8) of section 5 apply for the purposes of this section as they apply for the purposes of that.

(4) If the accused gives a defence statement under this section he must give it during the period which, by virtue of section 12, is the relevant period for this section.

7 Secondary disclosure by prosecutor

(1) This section applies where the accused gives a defence statement under section 5 or 6.

(2) The prosecutor must –

(a) disclose to the accused any prosecution material which has not previously been disclosed to the accused and which might be reasonably expected to assist the accused's defence as disclosed by the defence statement given under section 5 or 6, or

(b) give to the accused a written statement that there is no material of a description mentioned in paragraph (a).

(3) For the purposes of this section prosecution material is material –

(a) which is in the prosecutor's possession and came into his possession in connection with the case for the prosecution against the accused, or

(b) which, in pursuance of a code operative under Part II, he has inspected in connection with the case for the prosecution against the accused.

(4) Subsections (3) to (5) of section 3 (method by which prosecutor discloses) apply for the purposes of this section as they apply for the purposes of that.

(5) Material must not be disclosed under this section to the extent that the court, on an application by the prosecutor, concludes it is not in the public interest to disclose it and orders accordingly.

(6) Material must not be disclosed under this section to the extent that –

(a) it has been intercepted in obedience to a warrant issued under section 2 of the Interception of Communications Act 1985, or

(b) it indicates that such a warrant has been issued or that material has been intercepted in obedience to such a warrant.

(7) The prosecutor must act under this section during the period which, by virtue of section 12, is the relevant period for this section.

8 Application by accused for disclosure

(1) This section applies where the accused gives a defence statement under section 5 or 6 and the prosecutor complies with section 7 or purports to comply with it or fails to comply with it.

(2) If the accused has at any time reasonable cause to believe that –

(a) there is prosecution material which might be reasonably expected to assist the accused's defence as disclosed by the defence statement given under section 5 or 6, and

(b) the material has not been disclosed to the accused,

the accused may apply to the court for an order requiring the prosecutor to disclose such material to the accused.

(3) For the purposes of this section prosecution material is material –

(a) which is in the prosecutor's possession and came into his possession in connection with the case for the prosecution against the accused,

(b) which, in pursuance of a code operative under Part II, he has inspected in connection with the case for the prosecution against the accused, or

(c) which falls within subsection (4).

(4) Material falls within this subsection if in pursuance of a code operative under Part II the prosecutor must, if he asks for the material, be given a copy of it or be allowed to inspect it in connection with the case for the prosecution against the accused.

(5) Material must not be disclosed under this section to the extent that the court, on an application by the prosecutor, concludes it is not in the public interest to disclose it and orders accordingly.

(6) Material must not be disclosed under this section to the extent that –

(a) it has been intercepted in obedience to a warrant issued under section 2 of the Interception of Communications Act 1985, or

(b) it indicates that such a warrant has been issued or that material has been intercepted in obedience to such a warrant.

9 Continuing duty of prosecutor to disclose

(1) Subsection (2) applies at all times –

(a) after the prosecutor complies with section 3 or purports to comply with it, and

(b) before the accused is acquitted or convicted or the prosecutor decides not to proceed with the case concerned.

(2) The prosecutor must keep under review the question whether at any given time there is prosecution material which –

(a) in his opinion might undermine the case for the prosecution against the accused, and

(b) has not been disclosed to the accused;

and if there is such material at any time the prosecutor must disclose it to the accused as soon as is reasonably practicable.

(3) In applying subsection (2) by reference to any given time the state of affairs at that time (including the case for the prosecution as it stands at that time) must be taken into account.

(4) Subsection (5) applies at all times –

(a) after the prosecutor complies with section 7 or purports to comply with it, and

(b) before the accused is acquitted or convicted or the prosecutor decides not to proceed with the case concerned.

(5) The prosecutor must keep under review the question whether at any given time there is prosecution material which –

(a) might be reasonably expected to assist the accused's defence as disclosed by the defence statement given under section 5 or 6, and

(b) has not been disclosed to the accused;

and if there is such material at any time the prosecutor must disclose it to the accused as soon as is reasonably practicable.

(6) For the purposes of this section prosecution material is material –

(a) which is in the prosecutor's possession and came into his possession in connection with the case for the prosecution against the accused, or

(b) which, in pursuance of a code operative under Part II, he has inspected in connection with the case for the prosecution against the accused.

(7) Subsections (3) to (5) of section 3 (method by which prosecutor discloses) apply for the purposes of this section as they apply for the purposes of that.

(8) Material must not be disclosed under this section to the extent that the court, on an application by the prosecutor, concludes it is not in the public interest to disclose it and orders accordingly.

(9) Material must not be disclosed under this section to the extent that –

(a) it has been intercepted in obedience to a warrant issued under section 2 of the Interception of Communications Act 1985, or

(b) it indicates that such a warrant has been issued or that material has been intercepted in obedience to such a warrant.

10 Prosecutor's failure to observe time limits

(1) This section applies if the prosecutor –

(a) purports to act under section 3 after the end of the period which, by virtue of section 12, is the relevant period for section 3, or

(b) purports to act under section 7 after the end of the period which, by virtue of section 12, is the relevant period for section 7.

(2) Subject to subsection (3), the failure to act during the period concerned does not on its own constitute grounds for staying the proceedings for abuse of process.

(3) Subsection (2) does not prevent the failure constituting such grounds if it involves such delay by the prosecutor that the accused is denied a fair trial.

11 Faults in disclosure by accused

(1) This section applies where section 5 applies and the accused –

(a) fails to give a defence statement under that section,

(b) gives a defence statement under that section but does so after the end of the period which, by virtue of section 12, is the relevant period for section 5,

(c) sets out inconsistent defences in a defence statement given under section 5,

(d) at his trial puts forward a defence which is different from any defence set out in a defence statement given under section 5,

(e) at his trial adduces evidence in support of an alibi without having given particulars of the alibi in a defence statement given under section 5, or

(f) at his trial calls a witness to give evidence in support of an alibi without having complied with subsection (7)(a) or (b) of section 5 as regards the witness in giving a defence statement under that section.

(2) This section also applies where section 6 applies, the accused gives a defence statement under that section, and the accused –

(a) gives the statement after the end of the period which, by virtue of section 12, is the relevant period for section 6,

(b) sets out inconsistent defences in the statement,

(c) at his trial puts forward a defence which is different from any defence set out in the statement,

(d) at his trial adduces evidence in support of an alibi without having given particulars of the alibi in the statement, or

(e) at his trial calls a witness to give evidence in support of an alibi without having complied with subsection (7)(a) or (b) of section 5 (as applied by section 6) as regards the witness in giving the statement.

(3) Where this section applies –

(a) the court or, with the leave of the court, any other party may make such comment as appears appropriate;

(b) the court or jury may draw such inferences as appear proper in deciding whether the accused is guilty of the offence concerned.

(4) Where the accused puts forward a defence which is different from any defence set out in a defence statement given under section 5 or 6, in doing anything under subsection (3) or in deciding whether to do anything under it the court shall have regard –

(a) to the extent of the difference in the defences, and

(b) to whether there is any justification for it.

(5) A person shall not be convicted of an offence solely on an inference drawn under subsection (3).

(6) Any reference in this section to evidence in support of an alibi shall be construed in accordance with section 5.

12 Time limits

(1) This section has effect for the purpose of determining the relevant period for sections 3, 5, 6 and 7.

(2) Subject to subsection (3), the relevant period is a period beginning and ending with such days as the Secretary of State prescribes by regulations for the purposes of the section concerned.

(3) The regulations may do one or more of the following –

(a) provide that the relevant period for any section shall if the court so orders be extended (or further extended) by so many days as the court specifies;

(b) provide that the court may only make such an order if an application is made by a prescribed person and if any other prescribed conditions are fulfilled;

(c) provide that an application may only be made if prescribed conditions are fulfilled;

(d) provide that the number of days by which a period may be extended shall be entirely at the court's discretion;

(e) provide that the number of days by which a period may be extended shall not exceed a prescribed number;

(f) provide that there shall be no limit on the number of applications that may be made to extend a period;

(g) provide that no more than a prescribed number of applications may be made to extend a period;

and references to the relevant period for a section shall be construed accordingly.

(4) Conditions mentioned in subsection (3) may be framed by reference to such factors as the Secretary of State thinks fit.

(5) Without prejudice to the generality of subsection (4), so far as the relevant period for section 3 or 7 is concerned –

(a) conditions may be framed by reference to the nature or volume of the material concerned;

(b) the nature of material may be defined by reference to the prosecutor's belief that the question of non-disclosure on grounds of public interest may arise.

(6) In subsection (3) 'prescribed' means prescribed by regulations under this section.

13 Time limits: transitional

(1) As regards a case in relation to which no regulations under section 12 have come into force for the purposes of section 3, section 3(8) shall have effect as if it read –

'(8) The prosecutor must act under this section as soon as is reasonably practicable after –

(a) the accused pleads not guilty (where this Part applies by virtue of section 1(1)),

(b) the accused is committed for trial (where this Part applies by virtue of section 1(2)(a)),

(c) the proceedings are transferred (where this Part applies by virtue of section 1(2)(b) or (c)),

(d) the count is included in the indictment (where this Part applies by virtue of section 1(2)(d)), or

(e) the bill of indictment is preferred (where this Part applies by virtue of section 1(2)(e)).'

(2) As regards a case in relation to which no regulations under section 12 have come into force for the purposes of section 7, section 7(7) shall have effect as if it read –

'(7) The prosecutor must act under this section as soon as is reasonably practicable after the accused gives a defence statement under section 5 or 6.'

14 Public interest: review for summary trials

(1) This section applies where this Part applies by virtue of section 1(1).

(2) At any time –

(a) after a court makes an order under section 3(6), 7(5), 8(5) or 9(8), and

(b) before the accused is acquitted or convicted or the prosecutor decides not to proceed with the case concerned,

the accused may apply to the court for a review of the question whether it is still not in the public interest to disclose material affected by its order.

(3) In such a case the court must review that question, and if it concludes that it is in the public interest to disclose material to any extent –

(a) it shall so order, and

(b) it shall take such steps as are reasonable to inform the prosecutor of its order.

(4) Where the prosecutor is informed of an order made under subsection (3) he must act accordingly having regard to the provisions of this Part (unless he decides not to proceed with the case concerned).

15 Public interest: review in other cases

(1) This section applies where this Part applies by virtue of section 1(2).

(2) This section applies at all times –

(a) after a court makes an order under section 3(6), 7(5), 8(5) or 9(8), and

(b) before the accused is acquitted or convicted or the prosecutor decides not to proceed with the case concerned.

(3) The court must keep under review the question whether at any given time it is still not in the public interest to disclose material affected by its order.

(4) The court must keep the question mentioned in subsection (3) under review without the need for an application; but the accused may apply to the court for a review of that question.

(5) If the court at any time concludes that it is in the public interest to disclose material to any extent –

(a) it shall so order, and

(b) it shall take such steps as are reasonable to inform the prosecutor of its order.

(6) Where the prosecutor is informed of an order made under subsection (5) he must act accordingly having regard to the provisions of this Part (unless he decides not to proceed with the case concerned).

16 Applications: opportunity to be heard

Where –

(a) an application is made under section 3(6), 7(5), 8(5), 9(8), 14(2) or 15(4),

(b) a person claiming to have an interest in the material applies to be heard by the court, and

(c) he shows that he was involved (whether alone or with others and whether directly or indirectly) in the prosecutor's attention being brought to the material,

the court must not make an order under section 3(6), 7(5), 8(5), 9(8), 14(3) or 15(5) (as the case may be) unless the person applying under paragraph (b) has been given an opportunity to be heard.

17 Confidentiality of disclosed information

(1) If the accused is given or allowed to inspect a document or other object under –

(a) section 3, 4, 7, 9, 14 or 15, or

(b) an order under section 8,

then, subject to subsections (2) to (4), he must not use or disclose it or any information recorded in it.

(2) The accused may use or disclose the object or information –

(a) in connection with the proceedings for whose purposes he was given the object or allowed to inspect it,

(b) with a view to the taking of further criminal proceedings (for instance, by way of appeal) with regard to the matter giving rise to the proceedings mentioned in paragraph (a), or

(c) in connection with the proceedings first mentioned in paragraph (b).

(3) The accused may use or disclose –

(a) the object to the extent that it has been displayed to the public in open court, or

(b) the information to the extent that it has been communicated to the public in open court;

but the preceding provisions of this subsection do not apply if the object is displayed or the information is communicated in proceedings to deal with a contempt of court under section 18.

(4) If –

(a) the accused applies to the court for an order granting permission to use or disclose the object or information, and

(b) the court makes such an order,

the accused may use or disclose the object or information for the purpose and to the extent specified by the court.

(5) An application under subsection (4) may be made and dealt with at any time, and in particular after the accused has been acquitted or convicted or the prosecutor has decided not to proceed with the case concerned; but this is subject to rules made by virtue of section 19(2).

(6) Where –

(a) an application is made under subsection (4), and

(b) the prosecutor or a person claiming to have an interest in the object or information applies to be heard by the court,

the court must not make an order granting permission unless the person applying under paragraph (b) has been given an opportunity to be heard.

(7) References in this section to the court are to –

(a) a magistrates' court, where this Part applies by virtue of section 1(1);

(b) the Crown Court, where this Part applies by virtue of section 1(2).

(8) Nothing in this section affects any other restriction or prohibition on the use or disclosure of an object or information, whether the restriction or prohibition arises under an enactment (whenever passed) or otherwise.

18 Confidentiality: contravention

(1) It is a contempt of court for a person knowingly to use or disclose an object or information recorded in it if the use or disclosure is in contravention of section 17.

(2) The following courts have jurisdiction to deal with a person who is guilty of a contempt under this section –

(a) a magistrates' court, where this Part applies by virtue of section 1(1);

(b) the Crown Court, where this Part applies by virtue of section 1(2). Criminal Procedure and Investigations Act 1996, s 18

(3) A person who is guilty of a contempt under this section may be dealt with as follows –

(a) a magistrates' court may commit him to custody for a specified period not exceeding six months or impose on him a fine not exceeding £5,000 or both;

(b) the Crown Court may commit him to custody for a specified period not exceeding two years or impose a fine on him or both.

(4) If –

(a) a person is guilty of a contempt under this section, and

(b) the object concerned is in his possession,

the court finding him guilty may order that the object shall be forfeited and dealt with in such manner as the court may order.

(5) The power of the court under subsection (4) includes power to order the object to be destroyed or to be given to the prosecutor or to be placed in his custody for such period as the court may specify.

(6) If –

(a) the court proposes to make an order under subsection (4), and

(b) the person found guilty, or any other person claiming to have an interest in the object, applies to be heard by the court,

the court must not make the order unless the applicant has been given an opportunity to be heard.

(7) If –

(a) a person is guilty of a contempt under this section, and

(b) a copy of the object concerned is in his possession,

the court finding him guilty may order that the copy shall be forfeited and dealt with in such manner as the court may order.

(8) Subsections (5) and (6) apply for the purposes of subsection (7) as they apply for the purposes of subsection (4), but as if references to the object were references to the copy.

(9) An object or information shall be inadmissible as evidence in civil proceedings if to adduce it would in the opinion of the court be likely to constitute a contempt under this section; and 'the court' here means the court before which the civil proceedings are being taken.

(10) The powers of a magistrates' court under this section may be exercised either of the court's own motion or by order on complaint.

20 Other statutory rules as to disclosure

(1) A duty under any of the disclosure provisions shall not affect or be affected by any duty arising under any other enactment with regard to material to be provided to or by the accused or a person representing him; but this is subject to subsection (2).

(2) In making an order under section 9 of the Criminal Justice Act 1987 or section 31 of this Act (preparatory hearings) the judge may take account of anything which –

(a) has been done,

(b) has been required to be done, or

(c) will be required to be done,

in pursuance of any of the disclosure provisions. …

(5) For the purposes of this section –

(a) the disclosure provisions are sections 3 to 9;

(b) 'enactment' includes an enactment comprised in subordinate legislation (which here has the same meaning as in the Interpretation Act 1978).

21 Common law rules as to disclosure

(1) Where this Part applies as regards things falling to be done after the relevant time in relation to an alleged offence, the rules of common law which –

(a) were effective immediately before the appointed day, and

(b) relate to the disclosure of material by the prosecutor,

do not apply as regards things falling to be done after that time in relation to the alleged offence.

(2) Subsection (1) does not affect the rules of common law as to whether disclosure is in the public interest.

(3) References in subsection (1) to the relevant time are to the time when –

(a) the accused pleads not guilty (where this Part applies by virtue of section 1(1)),

(b) the accused is committed for trial (where this Part applies by virtue of section 1(2)(a)),

(c) the proceedings are transferred (where this Part applies by virtue of section 1(2)(b) or (c)),

(d) the count is included in the indictment (where this Part applies by virtue of section 1(2)(d)), or

(e) the bill of indictment is preferred (where this Part applies by virtue of section 1(2)(e)).

(4) The reference in subsection (1) to the appointed day is to the day appointed under section 1(5).

PART II

CRIMINAL INVESTIGATIONS

22 Introduction

(1) For the purposes of this Part a criminal investigation is an investigation conducted by police officers with a view to it being ascertained –

(a) whether a person should be charged with an offence, or

(b) whether a person charged with an offence is guilty of it.

(2) In this Part references to material are to material of all kinds, and in particular include references to –

(a) information, and

(b) objects of all descriptions.

(3) In this Part references to recording information are to putting it in a durable or retrievable form (such as writing or tape).

23 Code of practice

(1) The Secretary of State shall prepare a code of practice containing provisions designed to secure –

(a) that where a criminal investigation is conducted all reasonable steps are taken for the purposes of the investigation and, in particular, all reasonable lines of inquiry are pursued;

(b) that information which is obtained in the course of a criminal investigation and may be relevant to the investigation is recorded;

(c) that any record of such information is retained;

(d) that any other material which is obtained in the course of a criminal investigation and may be relevant to the investigation is retained;

(e) that information falling within paragraph (b) and material falling within paragraph (d) is revealed to a person who is involved in the prosecution of criminal proceedings arising out of or relating to the investigation and who is identified in accordance with prescribed provisions;

(f) that where such a person inspects information or other material in pursuance of a requirement that it be revealed to him, and he requests that it be disclosed to the accused, the accused is allowed to inspect it or is given a copy of it;

(g) that where such a person is given a document indicating the nature of information or other material in pursuance of a requirement that it be revealed to him, and he requests that it be disclosed to the accused, the accused is allowed to inspect it or is given a copy of it;

(h) that the person who is to allow the accused to inspect information or other material or to give him a copy of it shall decide which of those (inspecting or giving a copy) is appropriate;

(i) that where the accused is allowed to inspect material as mentioned in paragraph (f) or (g) and he requests a copy, he is given one unless the person allowing the inspection is of opinion that it is not practicable or not desirable to give him one;

(j) that a person mentioned in paragraph (e) is given a written statement that prescribed activities which the code requires have been carried out.

(2) The code may include provision –

(a) that a police officer identified in accordance with prescribed provisions must carry out a prescribed activity which the code requires;

(b) that a police officer so identified must take steps to secure the carrying out by a person (whether or not a police officer) of a prescribed activity which the code requires;

(c) that a duty must be discharged by different people in succession in prescribed circumstances (as where a person dies or retires).

(3) The code may include provision about the form in which information is to be recorded.

(4) The code may include provision about the manner in which and the period for which –

(a) a record of information is to be retained, and

(b) any other material is to be retained;

and if a person is charged with an offence the period may extend beyond a conviction or an acquittal.

(5) The code may include provision about the time when, the form in which, the way in which, and the extent to which, information or any other material is to be revealed to the person mentioned in subsection (1)(e).

(6) The code must be so framed that it does not apply to material intercepted in obedience to a warrant issued under section 2 of the Interception of Communications Act 1985.

(7) The code may –

(a) make different provision in relation to different cases or descriptions of case;

(b) contain exceptions as regards prescribed cases or descriptions of case.

(8) In this section 'prescribed' means prescribed by the code.

24 Examples of disclosure provisions

(1) This section gives examples of the kinds of provision that may be included in the code by virtue of section 23(5).

(2) The code may provide that if the person required to reveal material has possession of material which he believes is sensitive he must give a document which –

(a) indicates the nature of that material, and

(b) states that he so believes.

(3) The code may provide that if the person required to reveal material has possession of material which is of a description prescribed under this subsection and which he does not believe is sensitive he must give a document which –

(a) indicates the nature of that material, and

(b) states that he does not so believe.

(4) The code may provide that if –

(a) a document is given in pursuance of provision contained in the code by virtue of subsection (2), and

(b) a person identified in accordance with prescribed provisions asks for any of the material,

the person giving the document must give a copy of the material asked for to the person asking for it or (depending on the circumstances) must allow him to inspect it.

(5) The code may provide that if –

(a) a document is given in pursuance of provision contained in the code by virtue of subsection (3),

(b) all or any of the material is of a description prescribed under this subsection, and

(c) a person is identified in accordance with prescribed provisions as entitled to material of that description,

the person giving the document must give a copy of the material of that description to the person so identified or (depending on the circumstances) must allow him to inspect it.

(6) The code may provide that if –

(a) a document is given in pursuance of provision contained in the code by virtue of subsection (3),

(b) all or any of the material is not of a description prescribed under subsection (5), and

(c) a person identified in accordance with prescribed provisions asks for any of the material not of that description, the person giving the document must give a copy of the material asked for to the person asking for it or (depending on the circumstances) must allow him to inspect it.

(7) The code may provide that if the person required to reveal material has possession of material which he believes is sensitive and of such a nature that provision contained in the code by virtue of subsection (2) should not apply with regard to it –

(a) that provision shall not apply with regard to the material,

(b) he must notify a person identified in accordance with prescribed provisions of the existence of the material, and

(c) he must allow the person so notified to inspect the material.

(8) For the purposes of this section material is sensitive to the extent that its disclosure under Part I would be contrary to the public interest.

(9) In this section 'prescribed' means prescribed by the code.

25 Operation and revision of code ...

(3) A code brought into operation under this section shall apply in relation to suspected or alleged offences into which no criminal investigation has begun before the day so appointed. ...

26 Effect of code

(1) A person other than a police officer who is charged with the duty of conducting an investigation with a view to it being ascertained –

(a) whether a person should be charged with an offence, or

(b) whether a person charged with an offence is guilty of it,

shall in discharging that duty have regard to any relevant provision of a code which would apply if the investigation were conducted by police officers.

(2) A failure –

(a) by a police officer to comply with any provision of a code for the time being in operation by virtue of an order under section 25, or

(b) by a person to comply with subsection (1),

shall not in itself render him liable to any criminal or civil proceedings.

(3) In all criminal and civil proceedings a code in operation at any time by virtue of an order under section 25 shall be admissible in evidence.

(4) If it appears to a court or tribunal conducting criminal or civil proceedings that –

(a) any provision of a code in operation at any time by virtue of an order under section 25, or

(b) any failure mentioned in subsection (2)(a) or (b),

is relevant to any question arising in the proceedings, the provision or failure shall be taken into account in deciding the question.

27 Common law rules as to criminal investigations

(1) Where a code prepared under section 23 and brought into operation under section 25 applies in relation to a suspected or alleged offence, the rules of common law which –

(a) were effective immediately before the appointed day, and

(b) relate to the matter mentioned in subsection (2),

shall not apply in relation to the suspected or alleged offence.

(2) The matter is the revealing of material –

(a) by a police officer or other person charged with the duty of conducting an investigation with a view to it being ascertained whether a person should be charged with an offence or whether a person charged with an offence is guilty of it;

(b) to a person involved in the prosecution of criminal proceedings.

(3) In subsection (1) 'the appointed day' means the day appointed under section 25 with regard to the code as first prepared.

PART III

PREPARATORY HEARINGS

28 Introduction

(1) This Part applies in relation to an offence if –

(a) on or after the appointed day the accused is committed for trial for the offence concerned,

(b) proceedings for the trial on the charge concerned are transferred to the Crown Court on or after the appointed day, or

(c) a bill of indictment relating to the offence is preferred on or after the appointed day under the authority of section 2(2)(b) of the Administration of Justice (Miscellaneous Provisions) Act 1933 (bill preferred by direction of Court of Appeal, or by direction or with consent of a judge).

(2) References in subsection (1) to the appointed day are to such day as is appointed for the purposes of this section by the Secretary of State by order.

(3) If an order under this section so provides, this Part applies only in relation to the Crown Court sitting at a place or places specified in the order.

(4) References in this Part to the prosecutor are to any person acting as prosecutor, whether an individual or a body.

29 Power to order preparatory hearing

(1) Where it appears to a judge of the Crown Court that an indictment reveals a case of such complexity, or a case whose trial is likely to be of such length, that substantial benefits are likely to accrue from a hearing –

(a) before the jury are sworn, and

(b) for any of the purposes mentioned in subsection (2),

he may order that such a hearing (in this Part referred to as a preparatory hearing) shall be held.

(2) The purposes are those of –

(a) identifying issues which are likely to be material to the verdict of the jury;

(b) assisting their comprehension of any such issues;

(c) expediting the proceedings before the jury;

(d) assisting the judge's management of the trial.

(3) No order may be made under subsection (1) where it appears to a judge of the Crown Court that the evidence on an indictment reveals a case of fraud of such seriousness or complexity as is mentioned in section 7(1) of the Criminal Justice Act 1987 (preparatory hearings in cases of serious or complex fraud).

(4) A judge may make an order under subsection (1) –

(a) on the application of the prosecutor,

(b) on the application of the accused or, if there is more than one, any of them, or

(c) of the judge's own motion.

30 Start of trial and arraignment

If a judge orders a preparatory hearing –

(a) the trial shall start with that hearing, and

(b) arraignment shall take place at the start of that hearing, unless it has taken place before then.

31 The preparatory hearing

(1) At the preparatory hearing the judge may exercise any of the powers specified in this section.

(2) The judge may adjourn a preparatory hearing from time to time.

(3) He may make a ruling as to –

(a) any question as to the admissibility of evidence;

(b) any other question of law relating to the case.

(4) He may order the prosecutor –

(a) to give the court and the accused or, if there is more than one, each of them a written statement (a case statement) of the matters falling within subsection (5);

(b) to prepare the prosecution evidence and any explanatory material in such a form as appears to the judge to be likely to aid comprehension by the jury and to give it in that form to the court and to the accused or, if there is more than one, to each of them;

(c) to give the court and the accused or, if there is more than one, each of them written notice of documents the truth of the contents of which ought in the prosecutor's view to be admitted and of any other matters which in his view ought to be agreed;

(d) to make any amendments of any case statement given in pursuance of an order under paragraph (a) that appear to the judge to be appropriate, having regard to objections made by the accused or, if there is more than one, by any of them.

(5) The matters referred to in subsection (4)(a) are –

(a) the principal facts of the case for the prosecution;

(b) the witnesses who will speak to those facts;

(c) any exhibits relevant to those facts;

(d) any proposition of law on which the prosecutor proposes to rely;

(e) the consequences in relation to any of the counts in the indictment that appear to the prosecutor to flow from the matters falling within paragraphs (a) to (d).

(6) Where a judge has ordered the prosecutor to give a case statement and the prosecutor has complied with the order, the judge may order the accused or, if there is more than one, each of them –

(a) to give the court and the prosecutor a written statement setting out in general terms the nature of his defence and indicating the principal matters on which he takes issue with the prosecution;

(b) to give the court and the prosecutor written notice of any objections that he has to the case statement;

(c) to give the court and the prosecutor written notice of any point of law (including any point as to the admissibility of evidence) which he wishes to take, and any authority on which he intends to rely for that purpose.

(7) Where a judge has ordered the prosecutor to give notice under subsection (4)(c) and the prosecutor has complied with the order, the judge may order the accused or, if there is more than one, each of them to give the court and the prosecutor a written notice stating –

(a) the extent to which he agrees with the prosecutor as to documents and other matters to which the notice under subsection (4)(c) relates, and

(b) the reason for any disagreement.

(8) A judge making an order under subsection (6) or (7) shall warn the accused or, if there is more than one, each of them of the possible consequence under section 34 of not complying with it.

(9) If it appears to a judge that reasons given in pursuance of subsection (7) are inadequate, he shall so inform the person giving them and may require him to give further or better reasons.

(10) An order under this section may specify the time within which any specified requirement contained in it is to be complied with.

(11) An order or ruling made under this section shall have effect throughout the trial, unless it appears to the judge on application made to him that the interests of justice require him to vary or discharge it.

32 Orders before preparatory hearing

(1) This section applies where –

(a) a judge orders a preparatory hearing, and

(b) he decides that any order which could be made under section 31(4) to (7) at the hearing should be made before the hearing.

(2) In such a case –

(a) he may make any such order before the hearing (or at the hearing), and

(b) section 31(4) to (11) shall apply accordingly.

33 Crown Court Rules

(1) Crown Court Rules may provide that except to the extent that disclosure is required –

(a) by rules under section 81 of the Police and Criminal Evidence Act 1984 (expert evidence), or

(b) by section 5(7) of this Act,

anything required to be given by an accused in pursuance of a requirement imposed under section 31 need not disclose who will give evidence.

(2) Crown Court Rules may make provision as to the minimum or maximum time that may be specified under section 31(10).

34 Later stages of trial

(1) Any party may depart from the case he disclosed in pursuance of a requirement imposed under section 31.

(2) Where –

(a) a party departs from the case he disclosed in pursuance of a requirement imposed under section 31, or

(b) a party fails to comply with such a requirement,

the judge or, with the leave of the judge, any other party may make such comment as appears to the judge or the other party (as the case may be) to be appropriate and the jury may draw such inference as appears proper.

(3) In deciding whether to give leave the judge shall have regard –

(a) to the extent of the departure or failure, and

(b) to whether there is any justification for it.

(4) Except as provided by this section no part- –

(a) of a statement given under section 31(6)(a), or

(b) of any other information relating to the case for the accused or, if there is more than one, the case for any of them, which was given in pursuance of a requirement imposed under section 31,

may be disclosed at a stage in the trial after the jury have been sworn without the consent of the accused concerned.

35 Appeals to Court of Appeal

(1) An appeal shall lie to the Court of Appeal from any ruling of a judge under section 31(3), but only with the leave of the judge or of the Court of Appeal.

(2) The judge may continue a preparatory hearing notwithstanding that leave to appeal has been granted under subsection (1), but no jury shall be sworn until after the appeal has been determined or abandoned.

(3) On the termination of the hearing of an appeal, the Court of Appeal may confirm, reverse or vary the decision appealed against.

(4) Subject to rules of court made under section 53(1) of the Supreme Court Act 1981 (power by rules to distribute business of Court of Appeal between its civil and criminal divisions) –

(a) the jurisdiction of the Court of Appeal under subsection (1) above shall be exercised by the criminal division of the court;

(b) references in this Part to the Court of Appeal shall be construed as references to that division.

PART IV

RULINGS

39 Meaning of pre-trial hearing

(1) For the purposes of this Part a hearing is a pre-trial hearing if it relates to a trial on indictment and it takes place –

(a) after the accused has been committed for trial for the offence concerned or after the proceedings for the trial have been transferred to the Crown Court, and

(b) before the start of the trial.

(2) For the purposes of this Part a hearing is also a pre-trial hearing if –
Criminal Procedure and Investigations Act 1996, s 39

(a) it relates to a trial on indictment to be held in pursuance of a bill of indictment preferred under the authority of section 2(2)(b) of the Administration of Justice (Miscellaneous Provisions) Act 1933 (bill preferred by direction of Court of Appeal, or by direction or with consent of a judge), and

(b) it takes place after the bill of indictment has been preferred and before the start of the trial.

(3) For the purposes of this section the start of a trial on indictment occurs when a jury is sworn to consider the issue of guilt or fitness to plead or, if the court accepts a plea of guilty before a jury is sworn, when that plea is accepted; but this is subject to section 8 of the Criminal Justice Act 1987 and section 30 of this Act (preparatory hearings).

40 Power to make rulings

(1) A judge may make at a pre-trial hearing a ruling as to –

(a) any question as to the admissibility of evidence;

(b) any other question of law relating to the case concerned.

(2) A ruling may be made under this section –

(a) on an application by a party to the case, or

(b) of the judge's own motion.

(3) Subject to subsection (4), a ruling made under this section has binding effect from the time it is made until the case against the accused or, if there is more than one, against each of them is disposed of; and the case against an accused is disposed of if –

(a) he is acquitted or convicted, or

(b) the prosecutor decides not to proceed with the case against him.

(4) A judge may discharge or vary (or further vary) a ruling made under this section if it appears to him that it is in the interests of justice to do so; and a judge may act under this subsection –

(a) on an application by a party to the case, or

(b) of the judge's own motion.

(5) No application may be made under subsection (4)(a) unless there has been a material change of circumstances since the ruling was made or, if a previous application has been made, since the application (or last application) was made.

(6) The judge referred to in subsection (4) need not be the judge who made the ruling or, if it has been varied, the judge (or any of the judges) who varied it.

(7) For the purposes of this section the prosecutor is any person acting as prosecutor, whether an individual or a body.

PART VII

MISCELLANEOUS AND GENERAL

58 Orders in respect of certain assertions

(1) This section applies where a person has been convicted of an offence and a speech in mitigation is made by him or on his behalf before –

(a) a court determining what sentence should be passed on him in respect of the offence, or

(b) a magistrates' court determining whether he should be committed to the Crown Court for sentence.

(2) This section also applies where a sentence has been passed on a person in respect of an offence and a submission relating to the sentence is made by him or on his behalf before –

(a) a court hearing an appeal against or reviewing the sentence, or

(b) a court determining whether to grant leave to appeal against the sentence.

(3) Where it appears to the court that there is a real possibility that an order under subsection (8) will be made in relation to the assertion, the court may make an order under subsection (7) in relation to the assertion.

(4) Where there are substantial grounds for believing –

(a) that an assertion forming part of the speech or submission is derogatory to a person's character (for instance, because it suggests that his conduct is or has been criminal, immoral or improper), and

(b) that the assertion is false or that the facts asserted are irrelevant to the sentence, the court may make an order under subsection (8) in relation to the assertion.

(5) An order under subsection (7) or (8) must not be made in relation to an assertion if it appears to the court that the assertion was previously made –

(a) at the trial at which the person was convicted of the offence, or

(b) during any other proceedings relating to the offence.

(6) Section 59 has effect where a court makes an order under subsection (7) or (8).

(7) An order under this subsection –

(a) may be made at any time before the court has made a determination with regard to sentencing;

(b) may be revoked at any time by the court;

(c) subject to paragraph (b), shall cease to have effect when the court makes a determination with regard to sentencing.

(8) An order under this subsection –

(a) may be made after the court has made a determination with regard to sentencing, but only if it is made as soon as is reasonably practicable after the making of the determination;

(b) may be revoked at any time by the court;

(c) subject to paragraph (b), shall cease to have effect at the end of the period of 12 months beginning with the day on which it is made;

(d) may be made whether or not an order has been made under subsection (7) with regard to the case concerned.

(9) For the purposes of subsections (7) and (8) the court makes a determination with regard to sentencing –

(a) when it determines what sentence should be passed (where this section applies by virtue of subsection (1)(a));

(b) when it determines whether the person should be committed to the Crown Court for sentence (where this section applies by virtue of subsection Criminal Procedure and Investigations Act 1996, s 58 (1)(b));

(c) when it determines what the sentence should be (where this section applies by virtue of subsection (2)(a));

(d) when it determines whether to grant leave to appeal (where this section applies by virtue of subsection (2)(b)).

68 Use of written statements and depositions at trial

Schedule 2 to this Act (which relates to the use at the trial of written statements and depositions admitted in evidence in committal proceedings) shall have effect.

SCHEDULE 2

STATEMENTS AND DEPOSITIONS

1. – (1) Sub-paragraph (2) applies if –

(a) a written statement has been admitted in evidence in proceedings before a magistrates' court inquiring into an offence as examining justices,

(b) in those proceedings a person has been committed for trial,

(c) for the purposes of section 5A of the Magistrates' Courts Act 1980 the statement complied with section 5B of that Act prior to the committal for trial,

(d) the statement purports to be signed by a justice of the peace, and

(e) sub-paragraph (3) does not prevent sub-paragraph (2) applying.

(2) Where this sub-paragraph applies the statement may without further proof be read as evidence on the trial of the accused, whether for the offence for which he was committed for trial or for any other offence arising out of the same transaction or set of circumstances.

(3) Sub-paragraph (2) does not apply if –

(a) it is proved that the statement was not signed by the justice by whom it purports to have been signed,

(b) the court of trial at its discretion orders that sub-paragraph (2) shall not apply, or

(c) a party to the proceedings objects to sub-paragraph (2) applying.

(4) If a party to the proceedings objects to sub-paragraph (2) applying the court of trial may order that the objection shall have no effect if the court considers it to be in the interests of justice so to order.

2. – (1) Sub-paragraph (2) applies if –

(a) in pursuance of section 97A of the Magistrates' Courts Act 1980 (summons or warrant to have evidence taken as a deposition etc.) a person has had his evidence taken as a deposition for the purposes of proceedings before a magistrates' court inquiring into an offence as examining justices,

(b) the deposition has been admitted in evidence in those proceedings,

(c) in those proceedings a person has been committed for trial,

(d) for the purposes of section 5A of the Magistrates' Courts Act 1980 the deposition complied with section 5C of that Act prior to the committal for trial,

(e) the deposition purports to be signed by the justice before whom it purports to have been taken, and

(f) sub-paragraph (3) does not prevent sub-paragraph (2) applying.

(2) Where this sub-paragraph applies the deposition may without further proof be read as evidence on the trial of the accused, whether for the offence for which he was committed for trial or for any other offence arising out of the same transaction or set of circumstances.

(3) Sub-paragraph (2) does not apply if –

(a) it is proved that the deposition was not signed by the justice by whom it purports to have been signed,

(b) the court of trial at its discretion orders that sub-paragraph (2) shall not apply, or

(c) a party to the proceedings objects to sub-paragraph (2) applying.

(4) If a party to the proceedings objects to sub-paragraph (2) applying the court of trial may order that the objection shall have no effect if the court considers it to be in the interests of justice so to order. ...

CIVIL PROCEDURE ACT 1997

(1997 c 12)

7 Power of courts to make orders for preserving evidence, etc

(1) The court may make an order under this section for the purpose of securing, in the case of any existing or proposed proceedings in the court –

(a) the preservation of evidence which is or may be relevant, or

(b) the preservation of property which is or may be the subject-matter of the proceedings or as to which any question arises or may arise in the proceedings.

(2) A person who is, or appears to the court likely to be, a party to proceedings in the court may make an application for such an order.

(3) Such an order may direct any person to permit any person described in the order, or secure that any person so described is permitted –

(a) to enter premises in England and Wales, and

(b) while on the premises, to take in accordance with the terms of the order any of the following steps.

(4) Those steps are –

(a) to carry out a search for or inspection of anything described in the order, and

(b) to make or obtain a copy, photograph, sample or other record of anything so described.

(5) The order may also direct the person concerned –

(a) to provide any person described in the order, or secure that any person so described is provided, with any information or article described in the order, and

(b) to allow any person described in the order, or secure that any person so described is allowed, to retain for safe keeping anything described in the order.

(6) An order under this section is to have effect subject to such conditions as are specified in the order.

(7) This section does not affect any right of a person to refuse to do anything on the ground that to do so might tend to expose him or his spouse to proceedings for an offence or for the recovery of a penalty.

(8) In this section –

'court' means the High Court, and
'premises' includes any vehicle;

and an order under this section may describe anything generally, whether by reference to a class or otherwise.

APPENDIX

SEXUAL OFFENCES (PROTECTED MATERIAL) ACT 1997

(1997 c 39)

1 Meaning of 'protected material'

(1) In this Act 'protected material', in relation to proceedings for a sexual offence, means a copy (in whatever form) of any of the following material, namely –

(a) a statement relating to that or any other sexual offence made by any victim of the offence (whether the statement is recorded in writing or in any other form),

(b) a photograph or pseudo-photograph of any such victim, or

(c) a report of a medical examination of the physical condition of any such victim,

which is a copy given by the prosecutor to any person under this Act.

(2) For the purposes of subsection (1) a person is, in relation to any proceedings for a sexual offence, a victim of that offence if –

(a) the charge, summons or indictment by which the proceedings are instituted names that person as a person in relation to whom that offence was committed; or

(b) that offence can, in the prosecutor's opinion, be reasonably regarded as having been committed in relation to that person;

and a person is, in relation to any such proceedings, a victim of any other sexual offence if that offence can, in the prosecutor's opinion, be reasonably regarded as having been committed in relation to that person.

(3) In this Act, where the context so permits (and subject to subsection (4)) –

(a) references to any protected material include references to any part of any such material; and

(b) references to a copy of any such material include references to any part of any such copy.

(4) Nothing in this Act –

(a) so far as it refers to a defendant making any copy of –

(i) any protected material, or

(ii) a copy of any such material,

applies to a manuscript copy which is not a verbatim copy of the whole of that material or copy; or

(b) so far as it refers to a defendant having in his possession any copy of any protected material, applies to a manuscript copy made by him which is not a verbatim copy of the whole of that material.

2 Meaning of other expressions

(1) In this Act –

'contracted out prison' means a contracted out prison within the meaning of Part IV of the Criminal Justice Act 1991;

'defendant', in relation to any proceedings for a sexual offence, means any person charged with that offence (whether or not he has been convicted);

'governor', in relation to a contracted out prison, means the director of the prison;

'inform' means inform in writing;

'legal representative', in relation to a defendant, means any authorised advocate or authorised litigator (as defined by section 119(1) of the Courts and Legal Services Act 1990) acting for the defendant in connection with any proceedings for the sexual offence in question;

'photograph' and 'pseudo-photograph' shall be construed in accordance with section 7(4) and (7) of the Protection of Children Act 1978;

'prison' means any prison, young offender institution or remand centre which is under the general superintendence of, or is provided by, the Secretary of State under the Prison Act 1952, including a contracted out prison;

'proceedings' means (subject to subsection (2)) criminal proceedings;

'the prosecutor', in relation to any proceedings for a sexual offence, means any person acting as prosecutor (whether an individual or a body);

'relevant proceedings', in relation to any material which has been disclosed by the prosecutor under this Act, means any proceedings for the purposes of which it has been so disclosed or any further proceedings for the sexual offence in question;

'sexual offence' means one of the offences listed in the Schedule to this Act.

(2) For the purposes of this Act references to proceedings for a sexual offence include references to –

(a) any appeal or application for leave to appeal brought or made by or in relation to a defendant in such proceedings;

(b) any application made to the Criminal Cases Review Commission for the reference under section 9 or 11 of the Criminal Appeal Act 1995 of any conviction, verdict, finding or sentence recorded or imposed in relation to any such defendant; and

(c) any petition to the Secretary of State requesting him to recommend the exercise of Her Majesty's prerogative of mercy in relation to any such defendant.

(3) In this Act, in the context of the prosecutor giving a copy of any material to any person –

(a) references to the prosecutor include references to a person acting on behalf of the prosecutor; and

(b) where any such copy falls to be given to the defendant's legal representative, references to the defendant's legal representative include references to a person acting on behalf of the defendant's legal representative.

3 Regulation of disclosures by prosecutor

(1) Where, in connection with any proceedings for a sexual offence, any statement or other material falling within any of paragraphs (a) to (c) of section 1(1) would (apart from this section) fall to be disclosed by the prosecutor to the defendant –

(a) the prosecutor shall not disclose that material to the defendant; and

(b) it shall instead be disclosed under this Act in accordance with whichever of subsections (2) and (3) below is applicable.

(2) If –

(a) the defendant has a legal representative, and

(b) the defendant's legal representative gives the prosecutor the undertaking required by section 4 (disclosure to defendant's legal representative),

the prosecutor shall disclose the material in question by giving a copy of it to the defendant's legal representative.

(3) If subsection (2) is not applicable, the prosecutor shall disclose the material in question by giving a copy of it to the appropriate person for the purposes of section 5 (disclosure to unrepresented defendant) in order for that person to show that copy to the defendant under that section.

(4) Where under this Act a copy of any material falls to be given to any person by the prosecutor, any such copy –

(a) may be in such form as the prosecutor thinks fit, and

(b) where the material consists of information which has been recorded in any form, need not be in the same form as that in which the information has already been recorded.

(5) Once a copy of any material is given to any person under this Act by the prosecutor, the copy shall (in accordance with section 1(1)) be protected material for the purposes of this Act.

4 Disclosure to defendant's legal representative

(1) For the purposes of this Act the undertaking which a defendant's legal representative is required to give in relation to any protected material given to him under this Act is an undertaking by him to discharge the obligations set out in subsections (2) to (7).

(2) He must take reasonable steps to ensure –

(a) that the protected material, or any copy of it, is only shown to the defendant in circumstances where it is possible to exercise adequate supervision to prevent the defendant retaining possession of the material or copy or making a copy of it, and

(b) that the protected material is not shown and no copy of it is given, and its contents are not otherwise revealed, to any person other than the defendant, except so far as it appears to him necessary to show the material or give a copy of it to any such person –

(i) in connection with any relevant proceedings, or

(ii) for the purposes of any assessment or treatment of the defendant (whether before or after conviction).

(3) He must inform the defendant –

(a) that the protected material is such material for the purposes of this Act,

(b) that the defendant can only inspect that material, or any copy of it, in circumstances such as are described in subsection (2)(a), and

(c) that it would be an offence for the defendant –

(i) to have that material, or any copy of it, in his possession otherwise than while inspecting it or the copy in such circumstances, or

(ii) to give that material or any copy of it, or otherwise reveal its contents, to any other person.

(4) He must, where the protected material or a copy of it has been shown or given in accordance with subsection (2)(b)(i) or (ii) to a person other than the defendant, inform that person –

(a) that that person must not give any copy of that material, or otherwise reveal its contents –

(i) to any other person other than the defendant, or

(ii) to the defendant otherwise than in circumstances such as are described in subsection (2)(a); and

(b) that it would be an offence for that person to do so.

(5) He must, where he ceases to act as the defendant's legal representative at a time when any relevant proceedings are current or in contemplation –

(a) inform the prosecutor of that fact, and

(b) if he is informed by the prosecutor that the defendant has a new legal representative who has given the prosecutor the undertaking required by this section, give the protected material, and any copies of it in his possession, to the defendant's new legal representative.

(6) He must, at the time of giving the protected material to the new legal representative under subsection (5), inform that person –

(a) that that material is protected material for the purposes of this Act, and

(b) of the extent to which –

(i) that material has been shown by him, and

(ii) any copies of it have been given by him,

to any other person (including the defendant).

(7) He must keep a record of every occasion on which the protected material was shown, or a copy of it was given, as mentioned in subsection (6)(b).

5 Disclosure to unrepresented defendant

(1) This section applies where, in accordance with section 3(3), a copy of

any material falls to be given by the prosecutor to the appropriate person for the purposes of this section in order for that person to show that copy to the defendant under this section.

(2) Subject to subsection (3), the appropriate person in such a case is –

(a) if the defendant is detained in a prison, the governor of the prison or any person nominated by the governor for the purposes of this section; and

(b) otherwise the officer in charge of such police station as appears to the prosecutor to be suitable for enabling the defendant to have access to the material in accordance with this section or any person nominated by that officer for the purposes of this section.

(3) The Secretary of State may by regulations provide that, in such circumstances as are specified in the regulations, the appropriate person for the purposes of this section shall be a person of any description so specified.

(4) The appropriate person shall take reasonable steps to ensure –

(a) that the protected material, or any copy of it, is only shown to the defendant in circumstances where it is possible to exercise adequate supervision to prevent the defendant retaining possession of the material or copy or making a copy of it,

(b) that, subject to paragraph (a), the defendant is given such access to that material, or a copy of it, as he reasonably requires in connection with any relevant proceedings, and

(c) that that material is not shown and no copy of it is given, and its contents are not otherwise revealed, to any person other than the defendant.

(5) The prosecutor shall, at the time of giving the protected material to the appropriate person, inform him –

(a) that that material is protected material for the purposes of this Act, and

(b) that he is required to discharge the obligations set out in subsection (4) in relation to that material.

(6) The prosecutor shall at that time also inform the defendant –

(a) that that material is protected material for the purposes of this Act,

(b) that the defendant can only inspect that material, or any copy of it, in circumstances such as are described in subsection (4)(a), and

(c) that it would be an offence for the defendant –

(i) to have that material, or any copy of it, in his possession otherwise than while inspecting it or the copy in such circumstances, or

(ii) to give that material or any copy of it, or otherwise reveal its contents, to any other person,

as well as informing him of the effect of subsection (7).

(7) If –

(a) the defendant requests the prosecutor in writing to give a further copy of the material mentioned in subsection (1) to some other person, and

(b) it appears to the prosecutor to be necessary to do so –

(i) in connection with any relevant proceedings, or

(ii) for the purposes of any assessment or treatment of the defendant (whether before or after conviction),

the prosecutor shall give such a copy to that other person.

(8) The prosecutor may give such a copy to some other person where no request has been made under subsection (7) but it appears to him that in the interests of the defendant it is necessary to do so as mentioned in paragraph (b) of that subsection.

(9) The prosecutor shall, at the time of giving such a copy to a person under subsection (7) or (8), inform that person –

(a) that the copy is protected material for the purposes of this Act,

(b) that he must not give any copy of the protected material or otherwise reveal its contents –

(i) to any person other than the defendant, or

(ii) to the defendant otherwise than in circumstances such as are described in subsection (4)(a); and

(c) that it would be an offence for him to do so.

(10) If the prosecutor –

(a) receives a request from the defendant under subsection (7) to give a further copy of the material in question to another person, but

(b) does not consider it to be necessary to do so as mentioned in paragraph (b) of that subsection and accordingly refuses the request,

he shall inform the defendant of his refusal.

(11) Any regulations under subsection (3) shall be made by statutory instrument subject to annulment in pursuance of a resolution of either House of Parliament.

6 Further disclosures by prosecutor

(1) Where –

(a) any material has been disclosed in accordance with section 3(2) to the defendant's legal representative, and

(b) at a time when any relevant proceedings are current or in contemplation the legal representative either –

(i) ceases to act as the defendant's legal representative in circumstances where section 4(5)(b) does not apply, or

(ii) dies or becomes incapacitated,

that material shall be further disclosed under this Act in accordance with whichever of section 3(2) or (3) is for the time being applicable.

(2) Where –

(a) any material has been disclosed in accordance with section 3(3), and

(b) at a time when any relevant proceedings are current or in contemplation the defendant acquires a legal representative who gives the prosecutor the undertaking required by section 4,

that material shall be further disclosed under this Act, in accordance with section 3(2), to the defendant's legal representative.

7 Regulation of disclosures by Criminal Cases Review Commission

(1) Where, in connection with any relevant application made to the Criminal Cases Review Commission, any material falling within any of paragraphs (a) to (c) of section 1(1) would (apart from this section) fall to be disclosed by the Commission to the applicant –

(a) the Commission shall not disclose that material to the applicant; and

(b) it shall instead be disclosed under this Act in accordance with subsections (2) and (3).

(2) The following provisions, namely –

(a) section 3(2) to (5), and

(b) sections 4 to 6,

shall apply in connection with any disclosure by the Commission in relation to which subsection (1) above applies as they apply in connection with any disclosure by the prosecutor in relation to which section 3(1) applies.

(3) For the purposes of –

(a) subsection (1) above, and

(b) the operation, in connection with any such disclosure by the Commission, of the provisions applied by subsection (2) above,

references in this Act to the prosecutor and the defendant shall be read as references to the Commission and the applicant respectively.

(4) In this section –

(a) 'relevant application' means an application made to the Commission for the reference under section 9 or 11 of the Criminal Appeal Act 1995 of any conviction, verdict, finding or sentence of a court in proceedings for a sexual offence; and

(b) 'the applicant', in relation to a relevant application, means the person by or on whose behalf the application is made.

8 Offences

(1) Where any material has been disclosed under this Act in connection with any proceedings for a sexual offence, it is an offence for the defendant –

(a) to have the protected material, or any copy of it, in his possession otherwise than while inspecting it or the copy in circumstances such as are described in section 4(2)(a) or 5(4)(a), or

(b) to give that material or any copy of it, or otherwise reveal its contents, to any other person.

(2) Where any protected material, or any copy of any such material, has been shown or given to any person in accordance with section 4(2)(b)(i) or (ii) or section 5(7) or (8), it is an offence for that person to give any copy of that material or otherwise reveal its contents –

(a) to any person other than the defendant, or

(b) to the defendant otherwise than in circumstances such as are described in section 4(2)(a) or 5(4)(a).

(3) Subsections (1) and (2) apply whether or not any relevant proceedings are current or in contemplation (and references to the defendant shall be construed accordingly).

(4) A person guilty of an offence under this section is liable –

(a) on summary conviction, to imprisonment for a term not exceeding six months or a fine not exceeding the statutory maximum or both;

(b) on conviction on indictment, to imprisonment for a term not exceeding two years or a fine or both.

(5) Where a person is charged with an offence under this section relating to any protected material or copy of any such material, it is a defence to prove that, at the time of the alleged offence, he was not aware, and neither suspected nor had reason to suspect, that the material or copy in question was protected material or (as the case may be) a copy of any such material.

(6) The court before which a person is tried for an offence under this section may (whether or not he is convicted of that offence) make an order requiring him to return any protected material, or any copy of any such material, in his possession to the prosecutor.

(7) Nothing in subsection (1) or (2) shall be taken to apply to –

(a) any disclosure made in the course of any proceedings before a court or in any report of any such proceedings, or

(b) any disclosure made or copy given by a person when returning any protected material, or a copy of any such material, to the prosecutor or the defendant's legal representative;

and accordingly nothing in section 4 or 5 shall be read as precluding the making of any disclosure or the giving of any copy in circumstances falling within paragraph (a) or (as the case may be) paragraph (b) above.

9 Modification and amendment of other enactments

(1) In sections 5B to 5D of the Magistrates' Courts Act 1980 (which were inserted by the Criminal Procedure and Investigations Act 1996 and relate to evidence before examining justices), any reference to a copy of a document (within the meaning of the 1980 Act) being given by or on behalf of the prosecutor to each of the other parties, or any other party, to the proceedings in question shall be construed, in the case of any disclosure in relation to which section 3(1) above applies, as a reference to the document being disclosed under this Act in accordance with section 3(2) or (3) above.

(2) Despite section 20(1) of the Criminal Procedure and Investigations Act 1996 (disclosure provisions of the Act not affected by other statutory duties), section 3(3) to (5) of that Act (manner of disclosure) shall not apply in relation to any disclosure required by section 3, 7 or 9 of that Act if section 3(1) above applies in relation to that disclosure.

(3) Sections 17 and 18 of that Act (confidentiality of disclosed information) shall not apply to any material disclosed under this Act in accordance with section 3(2) or (3) above.

(4) At the end of section 1 of the Criminal Procedure and Investigations Act 1996 (application of Part I of that Act) there shall be added –

'(6) In this Part –

(a) subsections (3) to (5) of section 3 (in their application for the purposes of section 3, 7 or 9), and

(b) sections 17 and 18,

have effect subject to subsections (2) and (3) of section 9 of the Sexual Offences (Protected Material) Act 1997 (by virtue of which those provisions of this Act do not apply in relation to disclosures regulated by that Act).'

11 Short title, commencement and extent ...

(2) This Act shall come into force on such day as the Secretary of State may appoint by order made by statutory instrument.

(3) Nothing in this Act applies to any proceedings for a sexual offence where the defendant was charged with the offence before the commencement of this Act. ...

SCHEDULE

SEXUAL OFFENCES FOR PURPOSES OF THIS ACT

1. Any offence under any of the following provisions of the Sexual Offences Act 1956 –

(a) section 1 (rape);

(b) section 2 (procurement of a woman by threats);

(c) section 3 (procurement of a woman by false pretences);

(d) section 4 (administering drugs to obtain intercourse with a woman);

(e) section 5 (intercourse with a girl under the age of 13);

(f) section 6 (intercourse with a girl between the ages of 13 and 16);

(g) section 7 (intercourse with a mentally handicapped person);

(h) section 9 (procurement of a mentally handicapped person);

(i) section 10 (incest by a man);

(j) section 11 (incest by a woman);

(k) section 12 (buggery);

(l) section 14 (indecent assault on a woman); (m) section 15 (indecent assault on a man); and

(n) section 16 (assault with intent to commit buggery).

2. Any offence under section 128 of the Mental Health Act 1959 (intercourse with mentally handicapped person by hospital staff etc.).

3. Any offence under section 1 of the Indecency with Children Act 1960 (indecent conduct towards young child).

4. Any offence under section 54 of the Criminal Law Act 1977 (incitement by man of his grand-daughter, daughter or sister under the age of 16 to commit incest with him).

5. Any offence under section 1 of the Protection of Children Act 1978 or section 160 of the Criminal Justice Act 1988 (indecent photographs of children).

6. Any offence under section 1 of the Criminal Law Act 1977 of conspiracy to commit any of the offences mentioned in paragraphs 1 to 5.

7. Any offence under section 1 of the Criminal Attempts Act 1981 of attempting to commit any of those offences.

8. Any offence of inciting another to commit any of those offences.

INDEX

To complete your order, please fill in the form below:

Module	Books required	Quantity	Price	Cost
		Postage		
		TOTAL		

For UK, add 10% postage and packing (£10 maximum).
For Europe, add 15% postage and packing (£20 maximum).
For the rest of the world, add 40% for airmail.

ORDERING

By telephone to Mail Order at 0171 385 3377, with your credit card to hand

By fax to 0171 381 3377 (giving your credit card details).

By post to:

Old Bailey Press, 200 Greyhound Road, London W14 9RY.

When ordering by post, please enclose full payment by cheque or banker's draft, or complete the credit card details below.

We aim to despatch your books within 3 working days of receiving your order.

Name

Address

Postcode Telephone

Total value of order, including postage: £

I enclose a cheque/banker's draft for the above sum, or

charge my ☐ Access/Mastercard ☐ Visa ☐ American Express

Card number

☐☐☐☐ ☐☐☐☐ ☐☐☐☐ ☐☐☐☐

Expiry date ☐☐☐☐

Signature: ....Date: ....